0 5 10 15 20 miles
0 20 km.
E. Ger.
Poland
W. Ger.
Czech.
MAP AREA
U.S.S.R.
Switz.
Aust.
Hungary
Romania
Italy
Yugoslavia
Bulg.
Alb.
Gr.
Turkey
U. S. S. R.
Ukrainian S. S. R.
ROMANIA
Lubnja
Užok
Luh
Vyška
Husnyj
Nyžnja Roztoka
Suchyj
Čornoholova
Stryj
Tyšiv
Zadil's'kyj
Jalove
Polyšče
Kanora
Talamoš
Veretečiv
Nyžnij Studenyj
Verchnij Studenyj
Roztoka
Huklyvyj
Pylypec'
Podobovec'
Izky
Ploske
Verchnij Bystryj
Majdan
Ripynne
Tjuška
Mižhirja (Volove)
Prochudnyj
Veča
Svaljava
Obava
Pasika
Nyžnja Vyžnycja
Kosyno
Hlynjanec'
Šelestovo
Plavja
Rozsoš
Mukačevo
Imšady
Negrovec'
Koločava-Horb
Tereblja
Rika
Chustyeja
Bajlovo
Boržava
Ugoča
Kid'ovš
Berehovo
Mužijevo
Četovo
Olešnyk
Vynohradiv (Sevljuš)
Verjacja
Nove Selo
Pidvynohradiv
Chust
Nyžnje Selyšče
Nankovo
Danylove
Sokyrnycja
Šandrovo
Krajnykovo
Steblivka
Novoselycja
Teresva
Sol'nyj
Vil'chivci
Rus'ke Pole
Vyškovo
Tjačiv
Tysa
Batar
Cholmec'
Julivci
Dibrova
Verchnje Vodjane
Seredjne Vodjane
Apša
Sighet
Rozsiška
Kosivs'kyj Polik
Kosivs'ka Poljana
Rachiv
Roztoky
Bila Tysa
Čorna Tysa
Kvasy
Jasynja
Stebnyj
Lazeščyna
Dilove
Bilyj Potik
Vyšava
Szatmar
E. McC. '80

HOLZKIRCHEN IN DEN KARPATEN

WOODEN CHURCHES IN THE CARPATHIANS

Die Fotografien
Florian Zapletals
ausgewählt und eingeleitet von
Paul R. Magocsi

The photographs of
Florian Zapletal
selected and introduced by
Paul R. Magocsi

W. Braumüller · A-1092 Wien

Die Drucklegung dieses Buches wurde durch die großzügige Förderung der byzantinischen ruthenischen erzbischöflichen Provinz der Vereinigten Staaten von Amerika ermöglicht.

Publication of this volume was made possible through the generous support of the Byzantine Ruthenian Metropolitan Province of the United States.

Graph. Gestaltung: Ulrike Dietmayer.

Design: Ulrike Dietmayer.

Deutsche Übersetzung von Helga Haynes.

German translation: Helga Haynes.

ISBN 3 7003 0311 4

Satz: Manz Satz + Druck, A-1090 Wien
Reproarbeit und Druck: Novographic, A-1230 Wien

Printed in Austria

INHALT

CONTENTS

To Anna Sijková Čuvanová
who still lives in the traditional way

EINLEITUNG

Paul R. Magocsi

Dieses Buch enthält das fotografische Erbe Florian Zapletals, eines Journalisten und Kunsthistorikers, der in den Jahren unmittelbar nach dem 1. Weltkrieg die kulturellen Reichtümer des karpato-russinischen Volkes, das die östlichsten Teile seines neuen Landes, der Tschechoslowakei, bewohnte, entdeckte. Obwohl die 240 Schwarzweißfotos dieses Bandes nur einen Ausschnitt aus Zapletals Werk darstellen, so geben sie dennoch einen überwältigenden Einblick in die großartige russinische Holzarchitektur wie auch in das Leben im subkarpatischen Gebiet in den ersten Jahrzehnten unseres Jahrhunderts. Aber wo liegt dieses anscheinend so exotische Land, wer sind seine Bewohner, und wer ist Florian Zapletal?

Der 1. Weltkrieg hatte umwälzende Veränderungen in der politischen, gesellschaftlichen und wirtschaftlichen Struktur Europas hervorgebracht. Ende 1918 waren die vier großen Dynastien – die Habsburger, die Hohenzollern, die Romanows und

INTRODUCTION

Paul R. Magocsi

This book contains the photographic legacy of Florian Zapletal, a journalist and art historian who in the years just after World War I discovered the cultural riches of the Carpatho-Rusyn people living in the easternmost regions of his new country of Czechoslovakia. Although the 240 black and white photographs in this album represent only a sample of Zapletal's work, they provide nonetheless a stunning introduction to the glories of Rusyn wooden architecture as well as a glimpse into life in the Subcarpathian region in the early decades of this century. But where is this seemingly exotic land, who are its inhabitants, and who is Florian Zapletal?

World War I wrought cataclysmic changes in the political, social, and economic structure of Europe. By late 1918, the four great dynastic houses that had ruled most of the Continent since the Middle Ages – the Habsburgs, Hohenzollerns, Romanovs, and Ottomans – had been driven from power. New states were soon

die Ottomanen –, die seit dem Mittelalter über den größten Teil des Kontinents geherrscht hatten, von der Macht vertrieben worden. Neue Staaten sollten bald an ihre Stelle treten; aus der österreichisch-ungarischen Monarchie allein wurden sieben Staaten gebildet.

Eins dieser Länder war die Tschechoslowakei, zusammengestückelt aus den vormals innerhalb von Cisleithanien regierten Ländern Böhmen, Mähren und Schlesien und den von den Slowaken bewohnten Komitaten des alten ungarischen Königreichs. Tschechische und slowakische Führer, wie Tomáš G. Masaryk, Edvard Beneš und Milan Štefánik, hatten die Kriegsjahre in den westlichen Hauptstädten damit verbracht, die Unterstützung der Alliierten für das Ziel ihres eigenen unabhängigen Staates zu gewinnen. Im Laufe ihrer Bemühungen hörten sie völlig unerwartet von einem benachbarten slawischen Volk, den Karpato-Russinen, das auch in den neuen tschechoslowakischen Staat aufgenommen werden wollte. Dieser Antrag wurde von Frankreich, Großbritannien und den Vereinigten Staaten gebilligt, und im Herbst 1919 erkannte die Pariser Friedenskonferenz offiziell an, daß „das russinische Gebiet südlich der Karpaten" ein autonomer Teil der tschechoslowakischen Republik werden solle.

to replace them; from the Habsburg Austro-Hungarian Empire alone, seven countries were created.

One of these was Czechoslovakia, carved out of the former Austrian-ruled provinces of Bohemia, Moravia, and Silesia, and the Slovak-inhabited counties of the old Hungarian Kingdom. Czech and Slovak leaders like Tomáš G. Masaryk, Edvard Beneš, and Milan Štefánik, had spent the war years in western capitals lobbying hard to obtain Allied support for the idea of their own independent state. In the course of these efforts, they quite unexpectedly heard from a neighboring Slavic people, the Carpatho-Rusyns, who also asked to be included in the new Czechoslovak state. This proposal was approved by France, Britain, and the United States, and by the fall of 1919 the Paris Peace Conference officially recognized that "Rusyn territory south of the Carpathians" should become an autonomous part of the Czechoslovak Republic.

The Carpatho-Rusyns (also known as Carpatho-Russians, Carpatho-Ruthenians, or Carpatho-Ukrainians) had, like the Slovaks, lived for almost a millennium in the Carpathian mountain region of northern Hungary. Popular tradition held that the Rusyns had had an independent state in

Die Karpato-Russinen (auch bekannt als Karpato-Russen, Karpato-Ruthenen oder Karpato-Ukrainer) hatten – wie die Slowaken – fast ein Jahrtausend lang im karpatischen Bergland Nordungarns gelebt. Die Volkstradition glaubte, daß die Russinen im Früh-Mittelalter einen unabhängigen Staat gehabt hätten, und im Jahre 1849 gab es auch ein kurzes Experiment mit beschränkter Selbstverwaltung. Aber die große Mehrheit der 500.000 Russinen begann ihr eigenes ausgeprägtes politisches Dasein als Karpato-Rusland *(Podkarpatská Rus)* erst 1919.

Ungleich den Tschechen und Slowaken, die nach dem Westen orientierte Katholiken oder Protestanten waren, waren die Karpato-Russinen Ostchristen. Zur Zeit der Gegenreformation, Anfang des 17. Jahrhunderts, war die Treue der Russinen zum orthodoxen Glauben der ungarischen katholischen Hierarchie und anschließend der Regierung Grund zu großer Besorgnis geworden. Warum sollten diese „Abtrünnigen" außerhalb der Rechtsprechung der Staatskirche leben? Man war der Ansicht, daß die Konvertierung zum römischen Katholizismus untunlich war; man legte den Russinen statt dessen nahe, der griechisch-katholischen Kirche beizutreten. Das geschah auch, nachdem mehrere ihrer Priester im Jahre 1646 Rom die Treue ge-

the early Middle Ages and a brief experiment in limited self-government took place in 1849, but it was really not until 1919 that most of the half-million Rusyns received their own distinct political entity known as Subcarpathian Rus' (Podkarpatská Rus).

Unlike the Czechs and Slovaks, who were western-oriented Roman Catholics or Protestants, the Carpatho-Rusyns were eastern Christians. By the time of the Counter Reformation in the early seventeenth century, the Orthodox allegiance of the Rusyns had become an issue of great concern to the Hungarian Catholic hierarchy and subsequently to the government. Why should these "schismatics" live beyond the jurisdiction of the state church? It was felt that conversion to Roman Catholicism was impractical, so instead the Rusyns were urged to join the Greek Catholic Church, which came into being after several of their priests swore allegiance to Rome in 1646. The Greek Catholic Church maintained most of the traditions of Orthodoxy, that is, the use of the Old Slavonic liturgy, the Cyrillic alphabet, and the Julian calendar, as well as married priests and a reverence for the eastern saints depicted on the many icons that filled churches and homes. Greek Catholics also recognized the authority of the Pope and their priesthood was educated and jurisdictionally integrated

schworen hatten. Die griechisch-katholische Kirche behielt den größten Teil der orthodoxen Traditionen bei, d. h. die altslawische Liturgie, das kyrillische Alphabet und den julianischen Kalender und auch verheiratete Priester und die Verehrung der östlichen Heiligen, die auf den vielen Ikonen in Kirchen und Häuser abgebildet sind. Die griechischen Katholiken erkannten auch die Autorität des Papstes an. Ihre Priester waren innerhalb der Struktur der römisch-katholischen Kirche ausgebildet und integriert. Nicht alle Russinen wurden sofort griechisch-katholisch. Bis zur Mitte des 18. Jahrhunderts existierte die orthodoxe Kirche in bestimmten Gebieten Karpato-Ruslands weiter.

Hand in Hand mit dem allmählichen Sieg des griechischen Katholizismus ging ein Ansteigen des kulturellen Niveaus des Gebietes. Um die Gebote des griechischen Katholizismus bekannt zu machen, wurden Katechismen, Gebetbücher und Grammatiken gedruckt, Seminare und Schulen eröffnet. Gleichzeitig wurden zahlreiche Kirchen gebaut. Der Anstieg subkarpatischer architektonischer Tätigkeit im 18. Jahrhundert lief mit ähnlichen Entwicklungen in anderen Teilen der Habsburger-Monarchie parallel.

Während des ganzen 17. Jahrhunderts waren die Habsburger bei ihrem Bemühen,

within the Roman Catholic ecclesiastical structure. However, not all Rusyns became Greek Catholic at once, and the Orthodox Church continued to exist in certain areas of Subcarpathian Rus' until the mid-eighteenth century.

The eventual victory of Greek Catholicism was accompanied by a rise in the cultural standards of the region. In order to present the dictates of Greek Catholicism, catechisms, prayerbooks and grammars were printed, and seminaries and schools were opened. At the same time, numerous churches were constructed. This increase in Subcarpathian architectural activity during the eighteenth century paralleled similar developments in other parts of the Habsburg Empire.

Throughout the seventeenth century, the Habsburg rulers had been busily engaged in costly wars in an effort to drive the Turks out of the Empire and to quell the revolts of the independent-minded Hungarian Protestant princes from Transylvania. When by the first decade of the eighteenth century these two goals had been achieved, Habsburg rulers could rejoice by building churches, monasteries, and palaces in the Baroque style of architects like Johann Fischer von Erlach, Lucas von Hildebrandt, and Jacob Prandtauer that still dominate

die Türken aus dem Reich zu vertreiben und die Aufstände der unabhängig gesinnten ungarisch-protestantischen Fürsten von Siebenbürgen zu bezwingen, in kostspielige Kriege verwickelt. Als diese beiden Ziele im ersten Jahrzehnt des 18. Jahrhunderts erreicht waren, konnten die Habsburger triumphieren: Sie ließen Kirchen, Klöster und Paläste im Barockstil von Architekten, wie Johann Fischer von Erlach, Lucas von Hildebrandt und Jakob Prandtauer, erbauen. Baudenkmale, die heute noch die Städte und ländlichen Gegenden des östlichen Mitteleuropas beherrschen.

Derselbe Zeitabschnitt brachte auch Karpato-Rusland, das vom Habsburgisch-Siebenbürgischen Krieg verwüstet worden war, den Frieden. Die ortsansässigen Architekten – viele von ihnen sind bis in unsere Zeit unbekannt geblieben – konnten ihre Energie dem Bau von Dorfkirchen widmen, und zwar aus dem einzigen Baumaterial, das sie in Hülle und Fülle umgab – dem Holz der karpatischen Wälder.

Da sie in einem Gebiet tätig waren, das von östlichen und westlichen kulturellen Einflüssen geprägt war, überrascht es nicht, daß die von den subkarpatischen Baumeistern gewählten Modelle eine große Auswahl verschiedenartiger architektonischer Stile umfaßten. Aus dem Osten kam

the cities and rural landscapes of East-Central Europe.

This same period also brought peace to Subcarpathian Rus', which had been ravaged by the Habsburg-Transylvanian civil war. Local architects, many of whom still remain unknown, could devote their energies to the construction of village churches from the only material that surrounded them in abundance – the wood of the Carpathian forests.

Because they worked in an area marked by eastern and western cultural influences, it is not surprising that the models chosen by Subcarpathian builders provided a wide range of diverse architectural styles. From the east came the inspiration for central-domed churches (the Hutsul style), while from the west came the three-part basilica plan (the Boikian and Lemkian styles). To the latter might be added Baroque cupolas or sharply-pointed Gothic spires. The result was a group of variegated but harmoniously balanced wooden structures that blended in perfectly with the surrounding mountainous landscape.

The creative genius of these eighteenth-century Subcarpathian architects was not really discovered and appreciated until the twentieth century. After Subcarpathian Rus' and the neighboring Rusyn-

die Inspiration für die Kirche mit einer Hauptkuppel (der Hutsulstil), während der dreiteilige Basilikaplan (der Bojker- und Lemakstil) aus dem Westen kam. Dem letzteren könnte man Barockkuppeln oder spitze gotische Türme hinzufügen. Das Resultat: eine Reihe vielfältiger, aber harmonischer Holzbauten, die auf einzigartige Weise mit der gebirgigen Landschaft verschmelzen.

Die kreative Schöpferkraft dieser subkarpatischen Architekten des 18. Jahrhunderts wurde erst im 20. Jahrhundert richtig entdeckt und anerkannt. Nachdem Karpato-Rusland und das benachbarte, von Russinen bewohnte Prešov-Gebiet der nordöstlichen Slowakei ein Teil der Tschechoslowakei wurde, entsandte die Zentralregierung in Prag eine Reihe „östlicher" Experten und Beamte zur Bildung einer Verwaltung für die neuerworbenen Gebiete. Theoretisch sollte Karpato-Rusland zwar autonomes Gebiet werden und von ortsansässigen Russinen verwaltet werden; in der Praxis kam das aber im großen und ganzen nicht zustande.

Die kulturellen Bemühungen der Prager Regierung waren da erfolgreicher. Viele neue Schulen wurden gebaut, Hunderte von Büchern, Zeitungen, literarischen und akademischen Fachzeitschriften wurden

inhabited Prešov Region of northeastern Slovakia became part of Czechoslovakia, the central government in Prague dispatched a number of "eastern" experts and officials to establish an administration for the newly-acquired territories. In theory, Subcarpathian Rus' was to be granted autonomy and to have an administration staffed by local Rusyns, although, for the most part, this did not come about.

The cultural efforts of the Prague government were more successful. Many new schools were built, hundreds of books, newspapers, literary reviews, and scholarly journals began to appear, and the formerly prevailing illiteracy of the population was significantly reduced. In part, this happened because a small but dedicated group of Czech administrators, publicists, teachers, and scholars devoted their energies and talents to fostering Carpatho-Rusyn culture.

Historically, the Carpatho-Rusyns were not unknown to the Czech elite. In the first decade of the nineteenth century, the Czech linguist and patron saint of pan-Slavism, Josef Dobrovský, had written about them. Later, other nineteenth-century Czech and Slovak leaders like Jan Kollár, Pavel Šafárik, L'udovít Štúr, Karel Havlíček, and Milan Hodža commented on the fate of

herausgegeben, und das Analphabetentum in der Bevölkerung wurde beträchtlich vermindert. Teilweise geschah das, weil eine kleine, aber eifrige Gruppe tschechischer Verwalter, Publizisten, Lehrer und Akademiker Energie und Talent der Förderung karpatisch-russinischer Kultur widmeten.

Historisch gesehen waren die Karpato-Russinen der tschechischen Elite nicht unbekannt. Im ersten Jahrzehnt des 19. Jahrhunderts hatte Josef Dobrovský, der tschechische Linguist und Erzvater des Panslawismus, über sie geschrieben. Später schrieben andere tschechische und slowakische Führer des 19. Jahrhunderts, wie Jan Kollár, Pavel Šafárik, L'udovít Štúr, Karel Havlíček und Milan Hodža, über das Schicksal ihres verwandten slawischen Volkes, der Russinen; aber erst 1919, als Karpato-Rusland Teil der Tschechoslowakei wurde, nahmen beträchtliche Teile der tschechischen Öffentlichkeit die Russinen zur Kenntnis.

Aus relativer Ferne, in Böhmen und Mähren (Prag liegt etwa 700 Kilometer westlich), sahen die Tschechen Karpato-Rusland als exotisches Land mit Urwäldern und Hirten in volkstümlichen Trachten, die ein ländliches Leben führten, das sich seit dem Mittelalter nicht viel verändert hatte. Tatsäch-

their fellow Slavs, the Rusyns; but it was really not until 1919, when Subcarpathian Rus' became part of Czechoslovakia, that any significant portion of the Czech public became aware of Rusyns.

From relatively far-off Bohemia and Moravia (Prague is over 500 miles to the west), Czechs generally saw Subcarpathian Rus' as an exotic land of primeval forests and folk-costumed shepherds who followed a traditional agricultural and pastoral life style that had not changed much since medieval times. Indeed, this romantic image attracted many Czechs, perhaps bored with their own urban surroundings, to seek refuge as vacationers or as young boy scouts among the hills and valleys of the Carpathians.

Several Czech writers also turned to the region for inspiration. The foremost among them was Ivan Olbracht, who wrote several essays and novels with a Rusyn background. The most famous is Nikola Šuhaj loupežník *(The Robber Nikola Šuhaj, 1933), about a modern Robin Hood of the Carpathians. Karel Čapek, another internationally acclaimed author, based his novel* Hordubal *(1933) on the tale of a Rusyn immigrant who returns to his homeland after toiling for several years in America. Literary works like these helped to correct the super-*

lich zog diese romantische Vorstellung viele von der eigenen städtischen Umgebung vielleicht gelangweilten Tschechen an, als Urlauber oder als junge Pfadfinder in den Hügeln und Tälern der Karpaten Zuflucht zu suchen.

Auch einige tschechische Schriftsteller suchten Inspiration in der Gegend, vor allem Ivan Olbracht, der mehrere Essays und Romane schrieb, der berühmteste „Nikola Šuhaj loupežník" (Der Räuber Nikola Šuhaj, 1933), eine Art moderner Robin Hood der Karpaten; auch Karel Čapek, ein international gefeierter Autor, der seinen Roman „Hordubal" (1933) auf der Geschichte eines russinischen Immigranten aufbaute, der nach einigen Jahren mühseliger Arbeit in Amerika in sein Heimatland zurückkehrt. Diese und ähnliche literarische Werke trugen dazu bei, das oberflächliche, romantisierte Bild der tschechischen Öffentlichkeit zu korrigieren, indem sie die harten wirtschaftlichen Umstände, unter denen die meisten Karpato-Russinen in Wirklichkeit lebten, zeigten.

Es war die Gelehrtenwelt, welche die meisten Werke über Karpato-Rusland herausbrachte. Innerhalb von nur zwei Jahrzehnten befaßten sich zahlreiche tschechische Gelehrte mit dem Studium aller Bereiche der russinischen Kultur und veröf-

ficially romantic way in which the Rusyns were viewed by the Czech public, revealing the harsh economic conditions under which most Carpatho-Rusyns actually lived.

But it was the world of scholarship which produced the largest number of writings on Subcarpathian Rus'. Within merely two decades, a host of Czech scholars studied all aspects of Rusyn culture and produced a remarkable number of publications, many of which continue to be of value today. In particular, four Czechs devoted almost all their scholarly efforts to Subcarpathian subjects: the historian František Gabriel (b. 1901), the literary and cultural historians Antonín Hartl (1885–1944) and František Tichý (1886–1968), and the art historian and political essayist Florian Zapletal (1884–1969).

Florian Zapletal was born in 1884 in Bochoř, a village in Moravia, which at that time was an Austrian crownland within the Habsburg Empire. Between 1905 and 1910, he studied journalism at Charles University in Prague and art history at the University of Vienna. Like many young men of his generation, he was decisively affected by the outbreak of World War I in August 1914. He was immediately drafted into the Austro-Hungarian army and in October sent off to

fentlichten eine bemerkenswerte Anzahl an Schriften, von denen viele noch heute von Wert sind. Vier Tschechen insbesondere widmeten fast alle ihre akademischen Bemühungen subkarpatischen Themen: der Historiker František Gabriel (geb. 1901), die Literatur- und Kunsthistoriker Antonín Hartl (1885–1944) und František Tichý (1886–1968) und der Kunsthistoriker und politische Essayist Florian Zapletal (1884–1969).

Florian Zapletal wurde 1884 in Bochoř, einem Dorf in Mähren, das zu jener Zeit österreichisches Kronland innerhalb der Habsburger Monarchie war, geboren. Zwischen 1905 und 1910 studierte er Zeitungswissenschaften an der Karlsuniversität in Prag und Kunstgeschichte an der Wiener Universität. Wie viele junge Männer seiner Generation war er entscheidend vom Ausbruch des 1. Weltkrieges im August 1914 betroffen. Er wurde unverzüglich in die österreichisch-ungarische Armee eingezogen und im Oktober an die Ostfront geschickt, um gegen die Russen zu kämpfen, die zu der Zeit schon die Nordseite der Karpaten erreicht hatten. Zapletal, der im Süden des Gebirges in dem von Russinen bewohnten Gebiet Prešov, heute die östliche Slowakei, stationiert war, sah zum ersten Mal subkarpatische Holzkirchen. Er war so beeindruckt, daß er,

the eastern front to fight the Russians, who by then already had reached the northern side of the Carpathian Mountains. Stationed south of the mountains in the Rusyn-inhabited Prešov Region of what is now eastern Slovakia, Zapletal came across Subcarpathian wooden churches for the first time. He was so impressed that while artillery flew overhead (once a bullet tore the sleeve of his overcoat) he busily filled his sketch-book with drawings of the wooden structures. Then, like many other Habsburg soldiers of Slavic background, Zapletal surrendered to the Russians. On November 24, 1914, he crossed over the front line and subsequently spent the rest of the war years in Russia. There, at relative leisure, he was able to study first hand the great treasures of eastern Slavic art and architecture, to learn Russian, and to place his journalistic talents in the service of the Czechoslovak liberation movement.

When the war ended and the new Czechoslovak state that included Subcarpathian Rus' was created, the central government in Prague was in need of experts on "eastern matters". For this reason, in May 1919, the republic's founder-president, Tomáš G. Masaryk, appointed his former university student Florian Zapletal chief of the press service in Subcarpathian Rus'. For two years Zapletal served in this

während Artillerie über ihn hinwegflog (einmal zerriß eine Kugel den Ärmel seines Mantels), eifrig sein Skizzenbuch mit Zeichnungen der Holzbauten füllte. Dann ging Zapletal – wie viele andere Habsburger Soldaten slawischer Herkunft – zu den Russen über. Am 24. November überquerte er die Front und verbrachte die restlichen Kriegsjahre in Rußland. Dort – relativ müßig – konnte er die großen Schätze der ostslawischen Kunst und Architektur aus erster Hand studieren, Russisch lernen und sein journalistisches Talent in die Dienste der tschechoslowakischen Befreiungsbewegung stellen.

Als der Krieg zu Ende war und der neue tschechoslowakische Staat einschließlich Karpato-Rusland geschaffen wurde, brauchte die Zentralregierung in Prag Fachleute für „östliche Angelegenheiten". Aus diesem Grund ernannte Tomáš G. Masaryk, der Gründer-Präsident der Republik, im Mai 1919 seinen ehemaligen Universitätsstudenten Florian Zapletal zum Leiter des Pressedienstes in Karpato-Rusland. Zwei Jahre lang arbeitete Zapletal in dieser Funktion. Während dieser Zeit schrieb er zahlreiche Artikel über die politischen, wirtschaftlichen und kulturellen Bedingungen und sammelte viel dokumentarisches Material für weitere akademische Studien über Karpato-Rusland. Da seine Berichte

capacity. During that time he wrote numerous articles about political, economic, and cultural conditions, and gathered much documentary material for future scholarly studies about Subcarpathian Rus'. However, because his reports became increasingly critical of Czechoslovak government policy in the region, he resigned his press service post in July 1921 and returned to Prague.

Nevertheless, during the two years he had spent in Subcarpathian Rus' he had had considerable free time, and had made more than two dozen trips to the remotest corners of the province looking for examples of wooden architecture. Sometimes he traveled by car, but to reach many inaccessible villages, he was often forced to go by horse cart or on foot. The joys and tribulations associated with his efforts were poignantly expressed in a letter to his fiancée toward the end of his stay in May 1921:

> *Whenever possible, I ask the Governor [of Subcarpathian Rus'] for the car, but yesterday I had to go on foot, since the automobile would not have made it along the mountain road. I went as far as Kostryna by train. Then I went on foot in the worst heat from ten until one in the afternoon. It seemed that the sun would scorch me, but, on the other hand, the final prize was great. The church in Vyška is worth the effort.*

jedoch die tschechoslowakische Regierungspolitik in dem Gebiet immer schärfer kritisierten, gab er im Juli 1921 seinen Posten im Pressedienst auf und kehrte nach Prag zurück.

Aber in den zwei Jahren, die er in Karpato-Rusland verbrachte, hatte er viel freie Zeit und machte mehr als zwei Dutzend Reisen in die entferntesten Winkel der Provinz, wo er nach Beispielen von Holzbaukunst Ausschau hielt. Manchmal reiste er mit dem Auto, aber um in viele damit unerreichbare Dörfer zu kommen, war er oft gezwungen, mit der Kutsche zu fahren oder zu Fuß zu gehen. Die mit seinen Bemühungen verbundenen Freuden und Leiden sind eindringlich in einem Brief an seine Verlobte gegen Ende seines Aufenthalts im Mai 1921 geschildert:

> Wenn immer möglich, bitte ich den Gouverneur [von Karpato-Rusland] um den Wagen, aber gestern mußte ich zu Fuß gehen, da das Auto es auf der Bergstraße nicht geschafft hätte. Bis Kostryna bin ich mit dem Zug gefahren. Dann bin ich bei größter Hitze von zehn Uhr morgens bis ein Uhr nachmittags zu Fuß gegangen. Die Sonne hätte mich fast verbrannt, aber andererseits war der Preis großartig. Die Kirche in Vyška ist die Anstrengung wert. Neben der Kirche ist eine Quelle mit gutem, kalten Wasser. Da habe ich eine halbe Stunde gelegen. Ich hätte sie austrinken können . . . Auf

> *Right by the church is a spring of good, cold water. I lay beside it for half an hour. I would have drunk the whole thing . . . On my way back I bathed in the open air for the first time this summer. It was a delight. A mountain stream makes its way through piles of large rocks and in one place it falls about five meters. I crawled up under the waterfall, which in five minutes had rinsed me off so thoroughly that there was nothing to do but leave the water. I had the impression that several blacksmiths were pounding me on the back with hammers . . . And thus the whole tiring journey in this tropical heat ended happily. At least, I still feel good. I am working hard in order to accomplish as much as possible in a short time. I work in very difficult circumstances, because the objects which I photograph are very remote from each other and sometimes can be reached only by foot. But the results of this work please me a hundred times over. I already have a collection of photographs of which I am really proud, particularly when I recall how much sweat, work, and money I put into them.*

After returning to Prague in late 1921, Zapletal was associated with the military establishment of the new Czechoslovak state, first as an advisor to the General Staff, then from 1929 to 1939 in the war archives. He did not give up his interest in Subcarpathian Rus', however. He returned there for several weeks during the sum-

dem Rückweg habe ich zum ersten Mal in diesem Sommer im Freien gebadet. Es war herrlich. Ein Gebirgsfluß windet sich durch Haufen großer Felsen und fällt an einer Stelle ungefähr fünf Meter tief. Ich bin unter den Wasserfall gekrochen, der mich innerhalb von fünf Minuten so gründlich abgekühlt hatte, daß ich das Wasser verlassen mußte. Ich hatte das Gefühl, daß mir ein paar Schmiede mit Hämmern auf den Rücken schlugen ... Die ganze ermüdende Reise in tropischer Hitze endete also glücklich. Zumindest fühle ich mich noch immer gut. Ich arbeite hart, um soviel wie möglich in kurzer Zeit zu erreichen. Ich arbeite unter sehr schwierigen Bedingungen, da die Objekte, die ich fotografiere, sehr weit voneinander entfernt sind und manchmal nur zu Fuß zugänglich sind. Aber die Ergebnisse dieser Arbeit bringen mir hundertfache Freude. Ich habe bereits eine Sammlung von Fotografien, auf die ich sehr stolz bin, vor allem, wenn ich daran denke, wieviel Schweiß, Arbeit und Geld ich hineingesteckt habe.

Nachdem Zapletal Ende 1921 nach Prag zurückgekehrt war, arbeitete er für das Militär des neuen tschechoslowakischen Staates, zuerst als Ratgeber für den Generalstab, dann, von 1929 bis 1939, im Kriegsarchiv. Er gab sein Interesse an Karpato-Rusland jedoch nicht auf. Er kehrte für einige Wochen im Sommer 1923 und im Sommer 1925 dorthin zurück, um mehr

mers of 1923 and 1925 in order to make more photographs and to gather further data for the more than 150 articles which he published in the Czech press dealing with history, politics, socioeconomic questions, religion, architecture, and painting in the region. Having exhausted Subcarpathian subjects, his interests changed in the late 1920s to the art and ethnography of his native Moravia.

Zapletal did not lose interest in Rusyn problems, however, even despite the great political changes that were associated with World War II. In March 1939, Czechoslovakia ceased to exist and Subcarpathian Rus' was occupied by Hungary. Its status did not change until the Red Army arrived in late 1944 and the territory was soon incorporated into the Soviet Union as the Transcarpathian oblast of the Ukrainian Soviet Socialist Republic. However, those Carpatho-Rusyns living in northeastern Slovakia remained within the boundaries of a restored Czechoslovakia. Since 1961 that group has had its own museum and cultural center in Svidník, and two years before his death in 1969 Zapletal donated to that institution his incredibly rich collection of newspapers, journals, and rare books from interwar Subcarpathian Rus'.

In his personal archive in Prague he left more than 500 glass plates of photographs

Fotos zu machen und weitere Daten für die mehr als 150 Artikel zu sammeln, die er in der tschechischen Presse über Geschichte, Politik, sozialwirtschaftliche Fragen, Religion, Architektur und Malerei in dem Gebiet veröffentlichte. Nachdem er subkarpatische Themen erschöpft hatte, wandte sich sein Interesse Ende der zwanziger Jahre der Kunst und Volkskunde seines Heimatlandes Mähren zu.

Zapletal verlor sein Interesse an russinischen Problemen jedoch selbst angesichts der mit dem 2. Weltkrieg verbundenen umwälzenden politischen Veränderungen nicht. Im März 1939 hörte die Tschechoslowakei auf zu existieren, und Karpato-Rusland wurde von Ungarn besetzt. Das änderte sich erst, als die Rote Armee Ende 1944 vorrückte. Das Gebiet wurde bald als transkarpatische Oblast der ukrainischen sozialistischen Sowjetrepublik in die Sowjetunion eingegliedert. Diejenigen Karpato-Russinen jedoch, die in der nordöstlichen Slowakei lebten, blieben innerhalb der Grenzen einer wiedererrichteten Tschechoslowakei. Seit 1961 hat diese Gruppe ihr eigenes Museum und kulturelles Zentrum in Svidník, und zwei Jahre vor seinem Tod im Jahre 1969 schenkte Zapletal dieser Institution seine unglaublich umfangreiche Sammlung an Zeitungen, Zeitschriften und seltenen Büchern vom Kar-

taken on his field trips throughout Subcarpathian Rus' in the early 1920s as well as his original German camera, "Compur", and his developing gear. Just before his wife died in 1973, she entrusted these materials to the Czechoslovak ethnographer Mykola Mušynka. Mušynka was so impressed by the aesthetic and technical quality of Zapletal's glass negatives that he extracted a representative collection and made them available to this author.

One immediate problem was how to arrange the photographs for this album. There were no adequate models to follow, since scholars have still not reached a consensus about the classification of Subcarpathian wooden architecture. Finally, it was decided to arrange the photographs according to geographic location; that is, according to the valleys of the various rivers and tributaries along which they are found. This seemed to be the most organic principle of classification, because rivers are always a basic means of economic and cultural communication. The map at the back of the book shows that the churches are clustered around 21 rivers and their tributaries; from east to west: Čorna and Bila Tysa, Kosivs'kyj Potik, Apša, Terešva, Tereblja, Sokyrnycja and Bajlovo, Chustycja, Rika, Tysa, Batar, Boržava, Veča, Latorycja, Ljuta, Už, Ondava, Toplja, Radomka,

pato-Rusland der Zwischenkriegsjahre.

In seinem Privatarchiv in Prag verblieben noch mehr als 500 Glasplatten von Fotografien, die er auf seinen Studienreisen durch Karpato-Rusland Anfang der zwanziger Jahre aufgenommen hatte. Sogar die deutsche Originalkamera „Compur" und das Entwicklungsgerät, das er benutzt hatte, waren noch da. Unmittelbar vor ihrem Tod im Jahre 1973 vertraute seine Frau dieses Material dem tschechoslowakischen Volkskundler Mykola Mušynka an. Mušynka war so von der ästhetischen und technischen Qualität der Glasnegative Zapletals beeindruckt, daß er eine repräsentative Auswahl daraus zusammen- und dem Verfasser zur Verfügung stellte.

Ein Problem war die Ordnung der Fotografien für diesen Bildband. Es existierten keine passenden Vorlagen, denen man folgen konnte, da sich die Gelehrten bis jetzt noch nicht über die Klassifizierung subkarpatischer Holzarchitektur einig geworden sind. Nach Inbetrachtziehung mehrerer Möglichkeiten wurde beschlossen, die Fotografien der geographischen Lage nach zu ordnen, d. h. nach den Tälern der verschiedenen Flüsse und Nebenflüsse, an denen sie sich befinden. Das schien das organischste Klassifizierungsprinzip zu

and Sekčov.

Like other classification systems, this one also has drawbacks. For instance, architecturally similar churches are frequently found in the valleys of different rivers. Moreover, the valley of a given river is often settled by different ethnographic and even national groups, and this may be reflected in the style of the wooden architecture. Nevertheless, considering the alternatives, the geographical approach seems to be the best resolution possible.

Zapletal recorded the churches from various points of view. As a rule he first gives a general view, followed by views of the side and rear, and finally he focuses on various architectural details – windows, doors, domes, thatched roofs, galleries, and eaves. He shows the binding of girders, the carving around doors and windows, the decorated pillars and arcades, and the subtle metalwork of the church crosses. In some cases he shows interior elements: iconostases, icons, and lecterns. Then again, he turns to the bell towers, the crosses, the gates, and the churchgrounds.

In some villages Zapletal "enlivens" the wooden architecture with photographs of Carpatho-Rusyns in traditional dress as well as examples of secular wooden archi-

sein, da die Flüsse immer die Hauptwege wirtschaftlicher und kultureller Kommunikation bildeten. Ein Blick auf die Karte im Vorsatz zeigt, daß die Objekte um 21 Flüsse und deren Nebenflüsse herum gruppiert sind; von Osten nach Westen: Čorna und Bila Tysa, Kosivs'kyj Potik, Apša, Terešva, Tereblja, Sokyrnycja und Bajlovo, Chustycja, Rika, Tysa, Batar, Boržava, Veča, Latorycja, Ljuta, Už, Ondava, Toplja, Radomka und Sekčov.

Wie andere Klassifizierungssysteme, hat auch dieses Nachteile. Beispielsweise werden, architektonisch gesehen, ähnliche Kirchen häufig in den Tälern verschiedener Flüsse gefunden. Weiterhin wird das Teil eines Flusses oft von verschiedenen ethnographischen und sogar verschiedenen Völkergruppen besiedelt, und das kann sich eventuell im Stil der Holzarchitektur widerspiegeln. Dennoch scheint die geographische Methode – in Anbetracht der anderen Möglichkeit – die beste Lösung des Klassifizierungsproblems zu sein.

Zapletal hat die Kirchen von verschiedenen Seiten her aufgenommen. Im allgemeinen gibt er zunächst eine allgemeine Ansicht, gefolgt von der Seiten- und Rückansicht, und schließlich lenkte er den Blick auf verschiedene architektonische Details – Fenster, Türen, Kuppeln, Strohdächer, Ga-

tecture: houses, bridges, wells, farm buildings, and so on. In this manner, the reader is taken on an artistic and ethnographic excursion through the Subcarpathian region, from the Čorna Tysa River in the far eastern Hutsul land to the Toplja Valley of Šariš county in the west.

All the photographs in this album were made from Zapletal's glass negatives. In the interest of preserving their original tone, they were retouched only slightly. Clearly, the photographic technology of the 1920s is not that of the present; nonetheless, we can admire both the artistic and the technical proficiency of his photographic work. The photographs are augumented by seven line drawings reproduced from V. Sičynskyj, Dřevěné stavby v Karpatské oblasti *(Prague, 1940).*

Each photograph is identified with the name of the village where it is located, the object, its date of construction, the date of the photograph (in parentheses), and in some instances indication if a church has been destroyed or transferred to another location. Despite extensive effort to establish dates of construction, this information is not available for several churches in the album. Lack of such information in contemporary sources suggests that many of the "undated" churches are no longer

lerien und Dachgesims. Er zeigt die Einfassung der Träger, das Schnitzwerk um Türen und Fenster herum, die verzierten Pfeiler und Arkaden und die feine Metallarbeit der Kirchenkreuze. In einigen Fällen zeigt er die inneren Elemente: Ikonostasen, Ikonen und Lesepulte. Dann wendet er sich wieder den Glockentürmen, Kreuzen, Toren und dem Kirchengelände zu.

In einigen Dörfern belebt Zapletal die Holzbaukunst mit Fotos von Karpato-Russinen in Volkstracht sowie Beispielen weltlicher Holzarchitektur: Häuser, Brücken, Brunnen, Farmgebäude usw. Auf diese Weise nimmt er den Leser auf einen künstlerischen und völkerkundlichen Ausflug durch die subkarpatische Gegend mit, vom Čorna-Tysa-Fluß in dem im äußersten Osten gelegenen Hutsulland bis zum Topljatal des Komitats Šariš im Westen.

Alle Fotografien in diesem Buch sind von Zapletals Glasnegativen angefertigt worden. Um den Originalton der Fotos beizubehalten, wurden sie nur leicht retuschiert. Die fotografische Technik der zwanziger Jahre ist offensichtlich nicht mit der heutigen zu vergleichen. Dennoch können wir sowohl das artistische als auch das technische Können seines fotografischen Werkes bewundern.

Jede Fotografie ist mit dem Namen des

standing today. Thus, Zapletal's photographs have become the only documentary legacy of their existence. Even for those still standing, the photographs as seen here are the best reproductions available in print. In order to have a better understanding of the style and structure of Subcarpathian wooden architecture, a brief essay on that subject by Florian Zapletal follows.

Dorfes, in dem sie aufgenommen wurde, dem Objekt, dem Erbauungsdatum, dem Datum der Fotografie (in Klammern) und in einigen Fällen mit dem Hinweis darauf, daß eine Kirche zerstört oder an einen anderen Ort verlegt worden ist, versehen. Trotz großer Bemühungen, die Baudaten zu bestimmen, fehlt diese Information für einige Kirchen in diesem Bildband. Das Fehlen solcher Angaben in modernen Quellen läßt vermuten, daß viele Kirchen „ohne Datum" heute nicht mehr stehen. Zapletals Fotos sind damit der einzige dokumentarische Beweis ihrer Existenz. Selbst für die noch bestehenden Kirchen sind die hier abgebildeten Fotografien die besten im Druck vorhandenen Reproduktionen. Zum besseren Verständnis des Stils und der Struktur der subkarpatischen Holzarchitektur schließt sich ein kurzer Aufsatz Florian Zapletals zu diesem Thema an.

DIE HOLZKIRCHEN DER KARPATO-RUSSINEN*

Florian Zapletal

Das von den Karpato-Russinen bewohnte Gebiet erstreckt sich entlang dem südlichen Kamm der Karpaten in einer Tiefe von nur 24 bis 64 km, aber über eine beträchtliche Länge von 480 km, und zwar vom Poprad (Fluß im Komitat Spiš) im Westen zur Vyšava (Fluß im Komitat Marmaroš) im Osten. Es ist in diesem Gebiet, daß eine große Anzahl, etwa 150, charakteristischer Holzkirchen erhalten geblieben sind. Diese Kirchen wären der Stolz, der Ruhm und die Freude eines jeden Volkes, ihre Schätze sind der Welt jedoch nicht bekannt (sie befinden sich noch nicht einmal in Igor Grabars eindrucksvoller „Geschichte der russischen Kunst"), und die heutigen Russinen schätzen sie wenig, wenn überhaupt und ersetzen sie, wo immer es möglich ist, durch neue, banale Steingebäude.

* Übertragen aus Florian Zapletals „Dřevěné chrámy Jihokarpatských Rusínů" erschienen in Josef Chmelař et. al. „Podkarpatská Rus" (Prag: Orbis, 1923), Seiten 117–121.

*THE WOODEN CHURCHES OF THE CARPATHO-RUSYNS**

Florian Zapletal

The territory inhabited by Carpatho-Rusyns extends along the southern crest of the Carpathian Mountains at a depth of only 15 to 40 miles but at a considerable length of 300 miles from the Poprad River (Spiš county) in the west to the Vyšava River (Maramaroš county) in the east. It is here that a large number of distinctive wooden churches, about 150, have been preserved. These churches would be the pride, glory, and joy of any people, but their treasures are unknown to the world (they are not even in Igor Grabar's monumental History of Russian Art*), while present-day Rusyns value them little, if at all, replacing them wherever possible by new banal stone structures.*

The territory of the Carpatho-Rusyns – from Spiš to Marmaroš counties – is situat-

* *Translated by Michael Bourke from Florian Zapletal, "Dřevěné chrámy Jihokarpatských Rusínů", in Josef Chmelař et. al.,* Podkarpatská Rus *(Prague, 1923), pp. 117–121.*

Das Gebiet der Karpato-Russinen – vom Komitat Spiš zum Komitat Marmaroš – liegt an der Grenze zweier verschiedener Kulturen: der westlichen, die in der großen Donauebene im Südwesten beginnt, und die östliche, die sich vom Nordosten über die Karpaten erstreckt. In unserem Gebiet prallen diese zwei Kulturen jedoch nicht aufeinander, sondern vermischen sich vielmehr, und dies wird am besten in der Architektur der Holzkirchen deutlich. Die westliche Steinarchitektur kommt am Fuße der Karpaten zum Einhalt oder reicht im äußersten Falle bis zum Vorgebirge der Karpaten, während im Gebirge selbst die russinische Holzarchitektur vorherrscht. Es gibt eine Gruppe von Holzkirchen, deren Herkunft und Formen nicht erklärt werden können, ohne den starken Einfluß des gotischen Stils zu berücksichtigen. Es gibt auch eine Gruppe von Kirchen, die auf flüchtiges Hinsehen einen barocken Einfluß erkennen lassen. Aber es gibt auch Kirchen, die den ausgeprägten östlichen Stil in der reinsten Form beibehalten haben und von jeglichem westlichen Einfluß fast unberührt sind. Jede dieser Gruppen ist weiterhin in eine Anzahl von Varianten unterteilt, die von dem großartigen technischen und stilistischen Können der Volksarchitekten zeugen. Es gibt keine zwei Kirchen, die völlig gleich sind. Ein allge-

ed on the boundary between two different cultures: the western, which begins from the great Danubian plain in the southwest; and the eastern, which spreads across the Carpathians from the northeast. However, in our territory these two cultures do not clash violently, but rather intermingle, and this can best be seen in the architecture of the wooden churches. The western, stone architecture stops at the foot of the Carpathians, or at most, reaches only as far as the Carpathian foothills, while the mountains themselves are dominated almost exclusively by wooden Rusyn architecture.

There is a whole group of wooden churches whose origins and forms cannot be explained without considering the intense influence of the Gothic style. There is also a group of churches which at a glance clearly show a Baroque influence. But there also are churches which have preserved the distinctive eastern style in its purest form, almost untouched by any western influence. Each of these groups is further differentiated into a number of variants, testifying to the great technical and stylistic ability of the folk builders. There is not a single church which would be completely identical to any other. A general type may exist, but there are kaleidoscopic differences in details, since there was a very

meiner Typ existiert vielleicht, aber es besteht eine ungeheure Vielfalt in bezug auf Details, da der Bereich der Möglichkeiten für den Geschmack des einzelnen Volksarchitekten weit gespannt war.

Es ist nicht richtig, die russinischen Holzkirchen (von denen die ältesten aus dem 17. Jahrhundert stammen) nach der Zahl ihrer Kuppeln zu klassifizieren. Die Berücksichtigung des Grundrisses ist ein zuverlässigeres Mittel. Folglich gibt es drei Grundtypen subkarpatischer Holzkirchen: 1. ein griechisches Kreuz mit Armen gleicher Länge und zentralem Grundriß; 2. drei ungleiche seitlich verbundene Quadrate oder Rechtecke, die von Osten nach Westen verlaufen und 3. ein rechteckiges Mittelschiff mit Raum für den Altar östlich davon. Der Grundriß, der Bau und die Ausschmückung der Kirchen kann natürlich viele Variationen und Übergangstypen aufweisen.

Die besten und reinsten Typen sind Typus 1 und 2. Im Hutsulland (an der oberen Tysa, von Jasynja bis Byčkov) finden wir Kirchen mit Zentralgrundriß. Ihr Zentrum besteht aus einem Quadrat, dessen vier Seiten aus gestalterischen Gründen organisch und symmetrisch mit rechteckigen Flügeln verbunden sind [Abb. 1]. Das sich daraus ergebende Viereck ist im Außenbau widergespiegelt. Auf das Viereck ist ein

wide range of possibilities for the individual preferences of the folk builders.

It is not correct to classify Rusyn wooden churches (the oldest examples of which date from the seventeenth century) according to the number of their cupolas. Consideration of the floor plan is more reliable. Consequently, there are three basic types of Subcarpathian wooden churches: 1. a centrally planned Greek cross with arms of equal length; 2. three unequal squares or rectangles, joined side by side in a line running from east to west; and 3. a rectangular nave with a place for the altar on its eastern side. Of course, the floor plan, construction, and decoration of the churches can display many variations and transitional types.

The best and purest types are the first and second. In the land of the Hutsuls (on the upper Tysa River, from Jasynja to Byčkov) are found centrally planned churches. Their center consists of a square, whose four sides are for purposes of design connected organically and symmetrically with rectangular wings [illus. 1]. The resultant tetragon is reflected in the outer structure. Onto the tetragon is placed a low octagon, which turns into a pyramid-shaped roof with a miniature cupola. The rectangular wings of the church in Jasynja are two-sto-

niedriges Achteck gesetzt, das in ein pyramidenförmiges Dach mit einer Miniaturkuppel übergeht. Die rechteckigen Kirchenflügel in Jasynja sind zweistöckig und mit Giebel bildenden Satteldächern versehen, wobei sich auf jedem Giebel eine kleine Kuppel befindet. Die ganze Kirche wird von einem großen Pultdach überdeckt, das auf wunderschön geschnitzten hölzernen Sparrenköpfen ruht. Dieses Dach bildet einen Vorsprung und schützt dadurch den unteren Gebäudeteil vor schlechtem Wetter und gewährt den Gläubigen Zuflucht.

Einzigartig und von fast kindlicher Einfachheit in der Gestaltung ist der zweite Typ, der ausschließlich karpato-russinisch ist. Er wird im Gebiet der Bojker, d. h. im nordwestlichen Teil des Komitats Marmaroš und in den nördlichen Teilen der Komitate Bereg und Už, vorgefunden. Diese Gebäude bestehen aus drei quadratischen oder rechteckigen, Seite an Seite angeordneten Einheiten, die in ostwestlicher Richtung verlaufen [siehe Abb. 176]. Dieser Typ dient den Bedürfnissen des russinischen ostchristlichen Rituals, in dem eine Wand, Ikonostase genannt, den Altar vom Hauptschiff trennt, während eine zweite Schranke die Männer von den Frauen trennt, am besten. Der Altar befindet sich im östlichen Teil; die Männer stehen im

ried and are covered with ridged roofs to form gables, while on top of each gable there is a small cupola. The whole church is covered by a large pent roof that rests on beautifully carved wooden cantilevers from transverse beams. This roof extends out, protecting the lower part of the edifice from bad weather and providing shelter for the faithful.

Most distinctive and with an almost childlike simplicity of design, is the second type, which belongs exclusively to the Carpatho-Rusyns. It is found in the Boikian region, that is, in the northwestern part of Marmaroš county and in the northern sections of Bereg and Už counties. These structures consist of three square or oblong units standing side by side and running in a line from east to west [see illus. 176]. This type best serves the needs of Rusyn Eastern Christian ritual, in which a wall called the iconostasis separates the altar from the nave, while another barrier further separates the men from the women. The altar is located in the eastern part; the men stand in the central or middle part; and the women in the western part (hence its name babinec'*). This tripartite ground plan is also reflected in the exterior, in which three tall pyramid-like towers, usually of different sizes, graduate upwards in height [see illus. 175]. In this group of*

zentralen oder mittleren Teil und die Frauen im westlichen Teil (daher der Name *babinec'*). Dieser dreiteilige Grundriß spiegelt sich auch im äußeren Bau wider, bei dem drei hohe, pyramidenähnliche Türme, gewöhnlich verschiedener Größe, sich in steigender Größenordnung erheben [siehe Abb. 175]. Bei diesem Kirchentyp können wir eine gewisse Entwicklung feststellen: eine Progression von der ursprünglichen Form, bei der das Horizontale über das Vertikale herrscht (wie bei der Kirche von Suchyj, Abb. 175–180, in der Nähe des Užokpasses), bis zu Formen, die, beeinflußt von der barocken Bauweise, das Vertikale betonen (wie bei der Kirche in Ploske, Abb. 146–148). In diesen vom Barock beeinflußten Kirchen sind die unteren Teile der zentralen und westlichen Abschnitte von pittoresken Galerien auf geschnitzten Pfählen umrahmt. Die barocken Kuppeln sind in der Komplexität und künstlerischen Ausarbeitung der Silhouetten sehr eindrucksvoll.

Der dritte Typ subkarpatischer Kirchenarchitektur herrscht entlang der Tysa (Fluß im Komitat Ugoča) vor, im südlichen Teil der Komitate Marmaroš, Bereg und Už und auch bei den Lemaken im nördlichen Teil der Komitate Zemplin, Šariš und Spiš. Der Grundriß [siehe Abb. 246] besteht aus einem einzigen von einem Satteldach be-

churches we can see a certain evolution: a progression from the original form – in which the horizontal dominates over the vertical (as in the church of Sukhyj, illus. 175–180, near the Užok Pass) – to forms which under the influence of baroque construction emphasize the vertical (as in the church in Ploske, illus. 146–148). In these baroque-influenced churches the lower portions of the central and western sections are encircled with picturesque galleries on carved posts. Their baroque cupolas are very imposing in the complexity and elaboration of their silhouettes.

The third type of Subcarpathian church architecture predominates along the Tysa River in Ugoča county and in the southern part of Marmaroš, Bereg, and Už counties, as well as among the Lemkians in the northern part of Zemplin, Šariš, and Spiš counties. The ground plan [see illus. 246] consists of a single oblong covered by a gable roof. At its eastern end is attached a presbyterium, which tapers off gradually or sometimes forms a polygon. As a result, the roof of the presbyterium sometimes stands by itself or is joined to the gable roof of the nave.

The influence of Roman Catholic churches is clear. In Marmaroš, Ugoča, and Bereg counties, the influence of Gothic stone ar-

deckten Rechteck. Am östlichen Ende ist ein Presbyterium angefügt, das sich allmählich verjüngt oder manchmal auch ein Vieleck bildet. Folglich steht das Dach des Presbyteriums manchmal allein oder ist mit dem Satteldach des Mittelschiffs verbunden.

Der Einfluß der römisch-katholischen Kirchen ist deutlich. In den Komitaten Marmaroš, Ugoča und Bereg war der Einfluß der gotischen Steinbaukunst auf die Holzbaukunst so stark, daß russinische Kirchen nicht nur bestimmte einzelne Details der Bauweise und Ausschmückung vom gotischen Stil übernahmen, sondern in einigen Fällen (wie bei der Kirche zu Saldoboš, Abb. 71–74) vollkommen in dem Stil geschaffen wurden. Die Annahme, daß der gotische Typ der russinischen Kirche von deutschen Kolonisten fertig in dieses Gebiet gebracht wurde, ist falsch. Viele Beweise (besonders hinsichtlich von Grundrissen, die dem östlichen Ritus angepaßt wurden) sprechen dafür, daß dieser gotische Holzkirchentyp an Ort und Stelle entstanden ist und allmählich entwickelt wurde, obwohl offensichtlich unter dem Einfluß gotischer Steinbaukunst, die in der Tat von deutschen Einwanderern mitgebracht worden war. Die schlanken, zierlichen Kirchtürme dieser „gotischen" Kirchen haben nur Zierwert. Sie sind am Westende

chitecture on the wooden architecture was so strong that Rusyn churches did not merely adapt certain individual details of construction and decoration from the Gothic style, but in some cases (as in the church at Saldoboš, illus. 71–74), they were created entirely in that style. It is wrong to assume that the Gothic type of Rusyn church was brought in ready form to this territory by German colonists. There is much evidence (especially in ground plans adapted to the Eastern Rite) that this Gothic type of wooden church arose in situ *and was developed by degrees, although obviously under the influence of Gothic stone architecture, which was indeed brought by German immigrants. The slender, elegant steeples of these "Gothic" churches have only decorative significance. They are placed on the western end of the steep gable roof. Their plans are rectangular. Their open galleries and four small corner steeples (similar to certain Prague churches), which form a transition from the basic square of the steeple to its conical tip, are very subtly executed. Another very effective part of these churches are the low open galleries above the western entrance to the church.*

In a somewhat reduced, simplified, and childlike form, this Gothic type of Rusyn wooden church made its way up the Tysa

des steilen Satteldachs angebracht. Der Grundriß der Türme ist rechteckig. Die offenen Galerien und vier kleinen Ecktürmchen (ähnlich denen bestimmter Prager Kirchen), die einen Übergang bilden von dem Grundquadrat des Turmes zur kegelförmigen Spitze, sind sehr subtil ausgeführt. Ein anderer wirkungsvoller Teil dieser Kirchen sind die niedrigen offenen Galerien oberhalb des westlichen Kircheneingangs.

In leicht verkleinerter, vereinfachter und kindlicher Form fand dieser gotische Typ der russinischen Holzkirche seinen Weg die Tysa flußaufwärts bis in den nordwestlichen Winkel des Komitats Marmaroš (im Volove-Bezirk) und von dort aus in den Bezirk Svaljava des Komitats Bereg. Andererseits ist im südlichen Teil des Komitats Už und im Gebiet der Lemaken (die Komitate Spiš, Šariš und Zemplin) der barocke Einfluß stark, besonders in der Form der Kirchentürme, wie beispielsweise bei der Kirche zu Čornoholova [siehe Abb. 201 und 204].

Trotzdem können die drei Typen subkarpatischer Holzkirchen weder auf ein Gebiet begrenzt noch örtlich genau bestimmt werden. Folglich gibt es bei den Hutsulen Kirchen des Lemakentyps, bei den Lemaken Kirchen der Bojkergruppe,

River to the northwestern corner of Marmaroš county (the Volove district) and thence to the Svaljava district of Bereg county. On the other hand, in the southern part of Už county and in the area of the Lemkians (Spiš, Šariš, and Zemplin counties), the Baroque influence is strong, especially in the form of the steeples, as in the church at Čornoholova [*see illus. 201 and 204*].

Nevertheless, the three types of Subcarpathian wooden churches cannot be delimited territorially nor localized precisely. Hence among the Hutsuls, there are churches of the Lemkian type; among the Lemkians are churches of the Boikian group; while among the Boikians "Gothic" churches encroach from the Tysa valley. But when we classify the wooden churches according to their artistic qualities, we see that the most perfect examples of the centrally-planned type are found among the Hutsuls (in Jasynja); the best tripartite churches are in the Boikian territory; the most perfect forms and techniques for "Gothic" churches are found along the Tysa River (from Sighet to Chust); and that the "Baroque" churches are found mainly among the Lemkians.

From a technical standpoint, the best of the Subcarpathian wooden churches are

während bei den Bojken „gotische“ Kirchen die Grenze des Tysatals überschreiten. Wenn wir aber die Holzkirchen nach ihren künstlerischen Merkmalen einordnen, sehen wir die besten Beispiele für den Typ mit zentralem Grundriß bei den Hutsulen (in Jasynja), die besten dreigeteilten Kirchen im Gebiete der Bojken, die perfektesten Formen und Techniken für gotische Kirchen entlang der Tysa (von Sighet bis Chust), und die „Barockkirchen“ befinden sich hauptsächlich bei den Lemaken.

Von der Technik her sind die besten subkarpatischen Holzkirchen die aus Eiche gebauten gotischen, die sich im Chust-Gebiet und in der Nähe von Sighet befinden. Das Innere dieser Kirchen ist verziert. Malereien, die entweder der bloßen Verzierung gelten oder die Heiligen darstellen, schmücken Wände und Decken. Entweder sind sie direkt auf die Wand gemalt oder auf Leinwand, die später auf die Wände geklebt wurde.

In den meisten russinischen Kirchen sind die Verzierungen jedoch ins Holz geschnitzt. Es ist erstaunlich, was für eine Wirkung die Erbauer dieser Kirchen erzielen durch die Auswahl des Baumaterials, die Gebäudesilhouette, den plastischen Effekt, die Anordnung von Türen und Fenstern, die Einfassung der Kirchen mit offe-

the Gothic ones made from oak that are found in the Chust area and near Sighet. The interiors of these churches are decorated. The walls and ceilings have paintings that are either ornamental or depict the saints. They are either painted directly on the walls or on canvas that is then pasted onto the walls.

In most Rusyn churches, however, the decorative details are carved into the wood. It is amazing what effects the builders of these churches obtain in the selection of building materials, in the silhouette of the structure, in plastic effect, in the placement of doors and windows, in the trimming of churches with groundlevel open galleries supported by carved posts, with ornaments on doors and around the windows, with galleries on slender steeples, with picturesque clusters of shingled roofing on countless gables and fantastic cupolas, as well as filigree rooflets on the pyramids (as among the Boikians).

In the center of the church's interior, which is only poorly lit by small windows, there is a stucturally articulated "wall" called the iconostasis. In the Eastern Rite, the iconostasis separates the altar area from the nave and has three doors, the center one known as the "Royal Door". The iconostasis also has several rows of pictures

nen Galerien zu ebener Erde, die von geschnitzten Pfeilern gestützt sind, mit Verzierungen auf Türen und um die Fenster, mit Galerien auf schlanken Türmen, mit pittoresken Gruppen zahlloser schindelbedachter Giebel und eindrucksvoller Kuppeln sowie kleinen Filigrandächern auf den Pyramiden (wie zum Beispiel bei den Bojkern).

Im Zentrum des Kircheninnern, das nur schwach von kleinen Fenstern erhellt wird, befindet sich eine in der Struktur deutlich hervortretende Wand, Ikonostase genannt. Im östlichen Ritus trennt die Ikonostase den Altarbereich vom Hauptschiff und hat drei Türen, von denen die mittlere als die „kaiserliche Tür" bekannt ist. Auf der Ikonostase befinden sich auch mehrere Reihen von Heiligengemälden, die auf Holz gemalt sind und als Ikonen bekannt sind. Diese Heiligenbilder schmücken oft alle Wände der Kirche, und unter ihnen befinden sich einige seltene alte Exemplare. Feine Schnitzarbeit ist auch überall zu sehen: an den Altären, an den drei Türen der Ikonostase (besonders an der „kaiserlichen Tür"), an den Kerzenständern vor der Ikonostase, an den Ständern für die liturgischen Bücher (manchmal mit den schönsten Beispielen folkloristischer Stickerei bedeckt), an den hölzernen Kelchen, an den Kreuzen, an den hölzernen Kerzenhal-

of the saints painted on wood and known as icons. These holy pictures often adorn all the walls of the church and among them there are some rare old specimens. The delicate work of the carvers is also seen everywhere: on the altars, on the three doors of the iconostasis (especially on the Royal Door), on the candle holders in front of the iconostasis, on the stands for the liturgical books (sometimes covered by the most beautiful samples of folk embroidery), on the wooden chalices, on the crosses, on the wooden chandeliers, and on the pews. Beyond that, the innumerable forged crosses on the cupolas with their great variety of forms demonstrate the technical ability and artistic taste of the folk blacksmiths.

The bell tower is usually located apart from the church, or is built directly above the section called the babinec' *closest to the entrance. The self-standing bell towers sometimes reach imposing heights and monumental form. The Jasynia bell tower near the main railroad station* [see *illus. 6*] *has no equal in all of Subcarpathian Rus'. The lower portion consists of a cube, on top of which is placed an octagon, capped by an eight-sided pyramidal roof. The horizontal and vertical lines are in rhythmic equilibrium. The poetic bell towers in Obava between Mukačevo and Svaljava* [*illus. 159*] *are some of the most beautiful,*

tern und an den Kirchenbänken. Darüber hinaus zeugen die unzähligen geschmiedeten Kreuze auf den Kuppeln mit ihrem großen Formenreichtum vom technischen Können und künstlerischen Geschmack der Volksschmiede.

Der Glockenturm befindet sich gewöhnlich getrennt von der Kirche oder direkt über dem *babinec'* genannten Teil, dem Eingang am nächsten. Die freistehenden Glockentürme sind manchmal von beeindruckender Höhe und imposanter Form. Der Jasynia Glockenturm in der Nähe des Hauptbahnhofes [siehe Abb. 6] findet in ganz Karpato-Rusland nicht seinesgleichen. Der untere Teil besteht aus einem Würfel, auf dem sich ein Achteck befindet, das von einem achtseitigen, pyramidenförmigen Dach überdeckt wird. Die waagerechten und senkrechten Linien sind rhythmisch ausgewogen. Die romantischen Glockentürme in Obava zwischen Mukačevo und Svaljava [Abb. 159] gehören zu den schönsten, aber wie die Kirchen selbst sind sie von der Zerstörung bedroht. Auch die verzierten Holztore der Zäune, die Kirche und Friedhof umgeben, zum Beispiel in Dibrova und Serednje Vodjane [Abb. 26–28], sind eindrucksvoll.

Die Holzkirchen sind mit Recht auf einer das Dorf überschauenden Anhöhe gebaut –

but like the churches themselves they are threatened by destruction. Another impressive feature are the ornamented wooden doors of the fences which surround the church and cemetery, for example, in Dibrova and Serednje Vodjane [*illus. 26–28*].

The wooden churches are rightfully built on an elevation overlooking the town – thus closer to God and far away from daily cares. They sit among large, stately trees, which protect them from fires and storms. For the Carpatho-Rusyn, who holds dearly to the old traditions, the wooden church is not only the place where he worships his God, it is also a valuable cultural museum containing the centuries-old heritage of his ancestors. The old wooden churches of the Carpatho-Rusyns were built on the principle of beauty, as was the Slavonic Rite, but never on someone else's principle of beauty, never on a borrowed beauty, rather on their own particular intimate type of beauty.

The mystical gloom of the wooden church dimly lighted by small windows, the silvery tones of the bells, the moving liturgical songs, the yellow flickering candles, the austere, stone-like faces of the saints looking down from the icons, the complete submission of the faithful to God's will – all this in the wooden church creates an at-

somit Gott näher und weit entfernt vom täglichen Getriebe. Sie sind umgeben von großen, stattlichen Bäumen, die sie vor Brand und Sturm schützen. Für den Karpato-Russinen, der treu an den alten Traditionen festhält, ist die Holzkirche nicht nur der Ort, an dem er Gott verehrt, sie ist auch ein wertvolles Kulturmuseum, das das jahrhundertealte Erbe seiner Vorfahren enthält. Die alten Holzkirchen der Karpato-Russinen wurden nach dem Prinzip der Schönheit gebaut, wie es der slawonische Ritus befahl, aber nie nach dem Schönheitsprinzip eines Fremden, niemals nach einem geliehenen Schönheitsideal, vielmehr nach ihrem ureigenen Schönheitsideal.

Das mystische Dunkel der Holzkirche, schwach von kleinen Fenstern erhellt, der silbrige Glockenton, die bewegenden liturgischen Gesänge, die flackernden gelben Kerzen, die strengen steinernen Gesichter der Heiligen, die von den Ikonen herabsehen, die völlige Unterwerfung der Gläubigen unter den Willen Gottes – all dies schafft eine Atmosphäre in der Holzkirche, die uns zwingt, uns vor der schöpferischen Kraft des einfachen Russinen, der in Jahrhunderten unermüdlicher Arbeit diesen seltenen und immer noch unbekannten und ungewürdigten Schatz Weltkultur – die Holzkirche – geschaffen hat, zu verbeugen und ihr unsere Ehrerbietung zu erweisen.

mosphere compelling us to bow down and to pay tribute to the creative genius of the simple Rusyn, who through centuries of indefatigable work has created this rare yet still unknown and unappreciated treasure of world culture – the wooden church.

BILDTEIL PHOTOGRAPHS

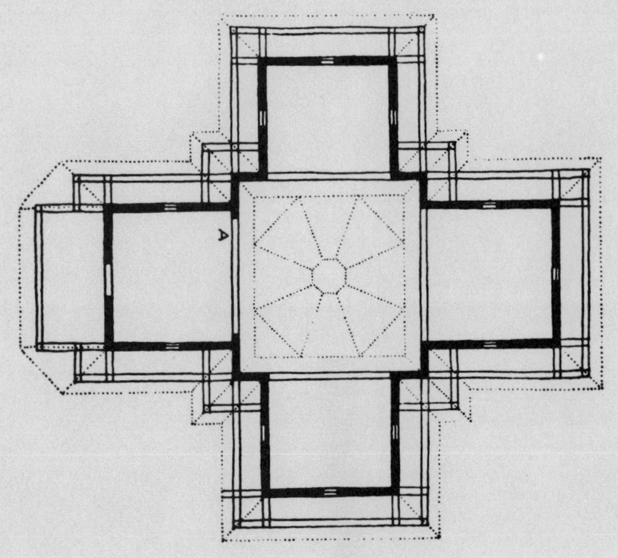

1 Jasynja. Grundriß. Auferstehungskirche (Struk Kirche), 1824.
Jasynja. Ground plan. Church of the Resurrection (Struk Church), 1824.

2 Jasynja. Auferstehungskirche (Struk Kirche) und Glockenturm, 1824 (1921).
Jasynja. Church of the Resurrection (Struk Church) and bell tower, 1824 (1921).

2

3 Jasynja. Frauen und Kinder in Hutsul Volkstracht (1920).
Jasynja. Women and children in Hutsul traditional dress (1920).

4 Jasynja. Mann in Hutsul Volkstracht (1920).
Jasynja. Man in Hutsul traditional dress (1920).

3

4

5 Jasynja. Auferstehungskirche (Struk Kirche), 1824 (1921).
Jasynja. Church of the Resurrection (Struk Church), 1824 (1921).

5

6

6 Jasynja. Auferstehungskirche (Struk Kirche) und Glockenturm, 1824 (1921).
Jasynja. Church of the Resurrection (Struk Church) and bell tower, 1824 (1921).

9 Lazeščyna. Kirche der Hl. Peter und Paul zu Plytovate, 18. Jhdt. (1921).
Lazeščyna. Church of Sts. Peter and Paul at Plytovate, 18th century (1921).

7 Jasynja. Frauen in Hutsul Volkstracht (1920).
Jasynja. Women in Hutsul traditional dress (1920).

8 Jasynja. Männer in Hutsul Volkstracht (1920).
Jasynja. Men in Hutsul traditional dress (1920).

7

8

12 Stebnyj. Kirche des Hl. Mulier (1921).
Stebnyj. Church of St. Mulier (1921).

10 Stebnyj. Kirche des Hl. Mulier (1921).
Stebnyj. Church of St. Mulier (1921).

10

11 Stebnyj. Kapelle (1921).
Stebnyj. Chapel (1921).

11

14 Roztoky. Kirche (1921).
Roztoky. Church (1921).

15 Roztoky. Kirche und Glockenturm (1921).
Roztoky. Church and bell tower (1921).

13 Kvasy. Kirche Mariä Geburt (1921).
Kvasy. Church of the Nativity of the Blessed Virgin Mary (1921).

13

14

15

17 Dilove (vormals Trebušany). Kirche Mariä Himmelfahrt, 1750 (1921).
Dilove (formerly Trebušany). Entrance, Church of the Ascension of the Virgin, 1750 (1921).

16 Bilyj Potik. Eingang, Kirche der Hl. Peter und Paul (1921).
Bilyj Potik. Entrance, Church of Sts. Peter and Paul (1921).

16

18

18 Dilove (vormals Trebušany). Kirche Mariä Himmelfahrt, 1750 (1921).
Dilove (formerly Trebušany). Church of the Ascension of the Virgin, 1750 (1921).

19 Dilove (vormals Trebušany). Kirche Mariä Himmelfahrt, 1750 (1921).
Dilove (formerly Trebušany). Church of the Ascension of the Virgin, 1750 (1921).

19

20 Kosivs'ka Poljana. Kirche der Hl. Peter und Paul (1921).
Kosivs'ka Poljana. Church of Sts. Peter and Paul (1921).

20

21

21 Rozsiška. Friedhofskreuze (1921).
Rozsiška. Crosses in the cemetery (1921).

24 Serednje Vodjane (vormals Serednja Apša). Kirche des Hl. Nikolaus, 17. Jhdt. (1921).
Serednje Vodjane (formerly Serednja Apša). Church of St. Nicholas, 17th century (1921).

22 Verchnje Vodjane (vormals Verchnja Apša). Friedhofskreuz (1921).
Verchnje Vodjane (formerly Verchnja Apša). Cemetery cross (1921).

22

23 Verchnje Vodjane (vormals Verchnja Apša). Kirche und Kreuz (1921).
Verchnje Vodjane (formerly Verchnja Apša). Church and cross (1921).

23

24

25

25 Dibrova (vormals Nyžnja Apša). Kirche des Hl. Basilius (1920).
Dibrova (formerly Nyžnja Apša). Church of St. Basil (1920).

28 Dibrova (vormals Nyžnja Apša). Kirche des Hl. Nikolaus, 18. Jhdt. (1920).
Dibrova (formerly Nyžnja Apša). Church of St. Nicholas, 18th century (1920).

26

26 Serednje Vodjane (vormals Serednja Apša). Portal zur Kirche des Hl. Nikolaus (1921).
Serednje Vodjane (formerly Serednja Apša). Portal to the Church of St. Nicholas (1921).

27 Serednje Vodjane (vormals Serednja Apša). Die Unterkirche (1921).
Serednje Vodjane (formerly Serednja Apša). The Lower Church (1921).

27

29 Dibrova (vormals Nyžnja Apša). Ausschnitt, Kirche des Hl. Basilius (1920).
Dibrova (formerly Nyžnja Apša). Detail, Church of St. Basil (1920).

29

30

30 Dibrova (vormals Nyžnja Apša). Frau Volkstracht (1920).
Dibrova (formerly Nyžnja Apša). Woman traditional dress (1920).

31 Novoselycja. Christi Himmelfahrt, 17. Jhdt. (1925).
Novoselycja. Church of the Ascension, 17th century (1925).

32 Novoselycja. Christi Himmelfahrt, 17. Jhdt. (1925).
Novoselycja. Church of the Ascension, 17th century (1925).

33 Novoselycja. Dachausschnitt, Christi Himmelfahrt, 17. Jhdt. (1925).
Novoselycja. Detail of roof, Church of the Ascension, 17th century (1925).

31

32

33

34

34 Sol'nyj. Kirche (1925).
Sol'nyj. Church (1925).

35 Vil'chivci (vormals Vul'chovci). Kircheneingang (1921).
Vil'chivci (formerly Vul'chovci). Entry to the Church (1921).

35

37

37 Negrovec'. Kirche des Erzengels Michael, 18. Jhdt. (1925).
Negrovec'. Church of the Archangel Michael, 18th century (1925).

36 Vil'chivci (vormals Vul'chovci). Kirche (1921).
Vil'chivci (formerly Vul'chovci). Church (1921).

36

38

38 Negrovec'. Holzbrücke (1925).
Negrovec'. Wooden bridge (1925).

40 Koločava-Horb. Heilig-Geist-Kirche, 18. Jhdt. (1925).
Koločava-Horb. Church of the Holy Ghost, 18th century (1925).

39 Negrovec'. Fassade und Veranda. Kirche des Erzengels Michael (1925).
Negrovec'. Façade and porch. Church of the Archangel Michael (1925).

39

41

41 Koločava-Horb. Kreuz am Wegesrand (1925).
Koločava-Horb. Wayside cross (1925).

42 Koločava-Horb. Fassade mit Galerie, Heilig-Geist-Kirche, 18. Jhdt. (1925).
Koločava-Horb. Façade with gallery, Church of the Holy Ghost, 18th century (1925).

42

44

44 Imšady. Glockenturm für die Kirche des Hl. Nikolaus (1925).
Imšady. Bell tower for the Church of St. Nicholas (1925).

43 Imšady. Fassade, Kirche des Hl. Nikolaus (1925).
Imšady. Façade, Church of St. Nicholas (1925).

43

45 Rus'ke Pole (vormals Velyke Urmezijevo). Kirche des Hl. Nikolaus (1925).
Rus'ke Pole (formerly Velyke Urmezijevo). Church of St. Nicholas (1925).

46 Rus'ke Pole (vormals Velyke Urmezijevo). Kirche des Hl. Nikolaus (1925).
Rus'ke Pole (formerly Velyke Urmezijevo). Church of St. Nicholas (1925).

46

47

48

49

47 Rus'ke Pole (vormals Male Urmezijevo). Kirche des Hl. Johannes des Täufers (1921).
Rus'ke Pole (formerly Male Urmezijevo). Church of St. John the Baptist (1921).

48 Rus'ke Pole (vormals Male Urmezijevo). Turmbasis, Kirche des Hl. Johannes des Täufers (1921).
Rus'ke Pole (formerly Male Urmezijevo). Base of tower, Church of St. John the Baptist (1921).

49 Rus'ke Pole (vormals Male Urmezijevo). Fassade, Kirche des Hl. Johannes des Täufers (1921).
Rus'ke Pole (formerly Male Urmezijevo). Façade, Church of St. John the Baptist (1921).

50 Danylove. Kirche des Hl. Nikolaus, 1779 (1921).
Danylove. Church of St. Nicholas, 1779 (1921).

52 Danylove. Fassade mit Galerie, Kirche des Hl. Nikolaus, 1779 (1921).
Danylove. Façade with gallery, Church of St. Nicholas, 1779 (1921).

50

51 Danylove. Turm, Kirche des Hl. Nikolaus, 1779 (1921).
Danylove. Tower, Church of St. Nicholas, 1779 (1921).

51

53 Danylove. Am Brunnen (1921).
Danylove. At the well (1921).

54 Šandrovo. Kirche der Hl. Paraskewa (1921).
Šandrovo. Church of St. Paraskeva (1921).

53

55

57 Krajnykovo. Kirche des Erzengels Michael, 1688 (1921).
Krajnykovo. Church of the Archangel Michael, 1688 (1921).

56 Krajnykovo. Dach, Kirche des Erzengels Michael, 1688 (1921).
Krajnykovo. Roof, Church of the Archangel Michael, 1688 (1921).

55 Krajnykovo. Glockenturm für die Kirche des Erzengels Michael (1921).
Krajnykovo. Bell tower for the Church of the Archangel Michael (1921).

56

58

58 Sokyrnycja. Kirche des Hl. Nikolaus, 1709 (1921).
Sokyrnycja. Church of St. Nicholas, 1709 (1921).

59 Sokyrnycja. Fassade mit Galerie, Kirche des Hl. Nikolaus, 1709 (1921).
Sokyrnycja. Façade with gallery, Church of St. Nicholas, 1709 (1921).

60

60 Nyžnje Selyšče. Kirche der Hl. Paraskewa (1925).
Nyžnje Selyšče. Church of St. Paraskeva (1925).

63 Nyžnje Selyšče. Eingang, Kirche der Hl. Paraskewa (1925).
Nyžnje Selyšče. Entrance, Church of St. Paraskeva (1925).

62 Nyžnje Selyšče. Kirche der Hl. Paraskewa (1925).
Nyžnje Selyšče. Church of St. Paraskeva (1925).

61

62

61 Nyžnje Selyšče. Fassade mit Galerie, Kirche der Hl. Paraskewa (1925).
Nyžnje Selyšče. Façade with gallery, Church of St. Paraskeva (1925).

63

64

65

64 Nyžnje Selyšče. Scheune und überdachter Heuschober (1925).
Nyžnje Selyšče. Barn and covered hay stack (1925).

65 Nankovo. Eckbalken, Haus (1925).
Nankovo. Corner joints, house (1925).

66 Tjačiv. Haus (1920).
Tjačiv. House (1920).

66

67

67 Tjačiv. Haus (1920).
Tjačiv. House (1920).

68 Vyškovo. Ev. Kirche (1925).
Vyškovo. Evangelical church (1925).

69 Vyškovo. Glockenstuhl, Ev. Kirche (1925
Vyškovo. Belfry, Evangelical churc (1925).

68

69

70 Vyškovo. Dorfhäuser (1925).
Vyškovo. Village houses (1925).

70

71

71 Steblivka (vormals Saldaboš). Rückseite, Marienkirche, 1780 (1925).
Steblivka (formerly Saldaboš). Rear, Church of the Virgin Mary, 1780 (1925).

72

73

72 Steblivka (vormals Saldaboš). Marienkirche, 1780 (1920).
Steblivka (formerly Saldaboš). Church of the Virgin Mary, 1780 (1920).

73 Steblivka (vormals Saldaboš). Marienkirche und Glockenturm, 1780 (1925).
Steblivka (formerly Saldaboš). Church of the Virgin Mary and bell tower, 1780 (1925).

74 Steblivka (vormals Saldaboš). Fassade mit Galerie, Marienkirche, 1643 (1925).
Steblivka (formerly Saldaboš). Façade with gallery, Church of the Virgin Mary, 1643 (1925).

74

75 Verjacja. Veranda eines Hauses (1925).
Verjacja. Veranda of a house (1925).

75

76

76 Verjacja. Haus (1925).
Verjacja. House (1925).

77 Pidvynohradiv (vormals Ardovec'). Glockenturm (1920).
Pidvynohradiv (formerly Ardovec'). Bell tower (1920).

78 Verjacja. Überdachte Kirchenpforte (1925).
Verjacja. Covered church gate (1925).

77

78

80 Olešnyk. Kruzifixbasis (1925).
Olešnyk. Base of crucifix (1925).

79 Olešnyk. Kruzifix (1925).
Olešnyk. Crucifix (1925).

79

80

81 Nove Selo. Kirche Mariä Geburt (1921).
Nove Selo. Church of the Nativity of the Virgin (1921).

82 Nove Selo. Kirche Mariä Geburt (1921).
Nove Selo. Church of the Nativity of the Virgin (1921).

81

82

83 Nove Selo. Kirche Mariä Geburt (1921).
Nove Selo. Church of the Nativity of the Virgin (1921).

83

85

85 Nove Selo. Hölzernes Glockenspiel der Osterzeremonie – klepač (1921).
Nove Selo. Easter ceremonial wooden chime–klepač (1921).

84 Nove Selo. Glockenturm für die Kirche Mariä Geburt (1921).
Nove Selo. Bell tower for the Church of the Nativity of the Virgin (1921).

84

86

86 Cholmec' (vormals Chlumec'). Allerheiligenkirche (1920).
Cholmec' (formerly Chlumec'). Church of All Saints (1920).

87 Cholmec' (vormals Chlumec'). Allerheiligenkirche (1920).
Cholmec' (formerly Chlumec'). Church of All Saints (1920).

87

88 Četovo. Ev. Kirche, 14. Jhdt. und Glockenturm, 18. Jhdt. (1921).
Četovo. Evangelical church, 14th century and bell tower, 18th century (1921).

88

89

89 Julivci (vormals Djula). Ev. Kirche (1925).
Julivci (formerly Djula). Evangelical church (1925).

91 Kid'ovš. Glockenturm (1925).
Kid'ovš. Bell tower (1925).

91

90

90 Mužijevo. Glockenturm (1921).
Mužijevo. Bell tower (1921).

92 Nyžnij Studenyj. Kirche des Hl. Nikolaus (1925).
Nyžnij Studenyj. Church of St. Nicholas (1925).

92

93

93 Nyžnij Studenyj. Glockenturm für die Kirche des Hl. Nikolaus (1925).
Nyžnij Studenyj. Bell tower for the Church of St. Nicholas (1925).

94

94 Verchnij Studenyj. Glockenturm der Himmelfahrtskirche (1925).
Verchnij Studenyj. Bell tower for the Church of the Ascension (1925).

95 Verchnij Studenyj. Himmelfahrtskirche (1925).
Verchnij Studenyj. Church of the Ascension (1925).

95

97 Roztoka. Nordseite. Kirche Mariä Opfer, 1759 (1925).
Roztoka. North side, Church of the Sacrifice of the Virgin, 1759 (1925).

97

96

96 Roztoka. Kirche Mariä Opfer 1759 (1925)
Roztoka. Church of the Sacrifice of the Virgin, 1759 (1925).

98 Roztoka. Glockenturm für die Kirche Mariä Opfer (1925).
Roztoka. Bell tower for the Church of the Sacrifice of the Virgin (1925).

99

99 Podobovec'. Turm, Kirche des Hl. Nik
laus, 1785 (1921).
Podobovec'. Tower, Church of St. Nich
las, 1785 (1921).

101 Podobovec'. Südseite, Kirche des Hl. Nikolaus, 1785 (1921).
Podobovec'. South side, Church of St. Nicholas, 1785 (1921).

100 Podobovec'. Kirche des Hl. Nikolaus un
Glockenturm, 1785 (1921).
Podobovec'. Church of St. Nicholas ar
bell tower, 1785 (1921).

100

102

102 Pylypec'. Glockenturm (1921).
Pylypec'. Bell tower (1921).

103 Pylypec'. Kirche Mariä Geburt, 1780 (1921).
Pylypec'. Church of the Nativity of the Virgin, 1780 (1921).

103

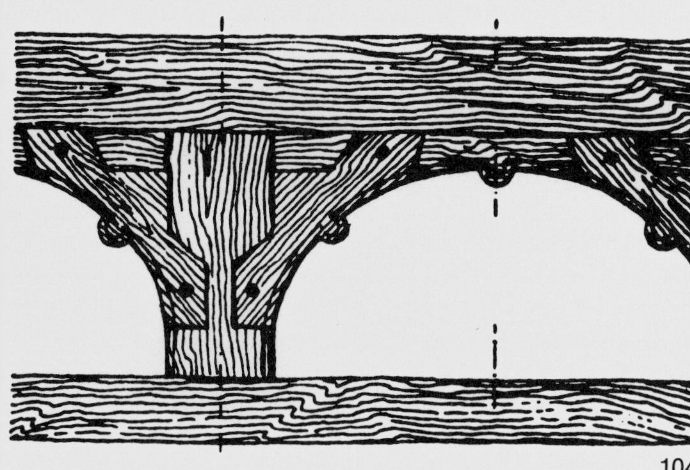

104 Pylypec'. Galeriebogen, Kirche Mariä Geburt, 1780.
Pylypec'. Gallery arch, Church of the Nativity of the Virgin, 1780.

105 Pylypec'. Fassade mit Galerie, Kirche Mariä Geburt, 1780 (1921).
Pylypec'. Façade with gallery, Church of the Nativity of the Virgin, 1780 (1921).

106

106 Roztoka. Eckbalken, Kirche Darstellung der Hl. Jungfrau Maria, 1759 (1925).
Roztoka. Corner joints, Church of the Presentation of the Virgin, 1759 (1925).

107 Pylypec'. Eingang, Kirche Mariä Geburt, 1780 (1921).
Pylypec'. Entrance, Church of the Nativity of the Virgin, 1780 (1921).

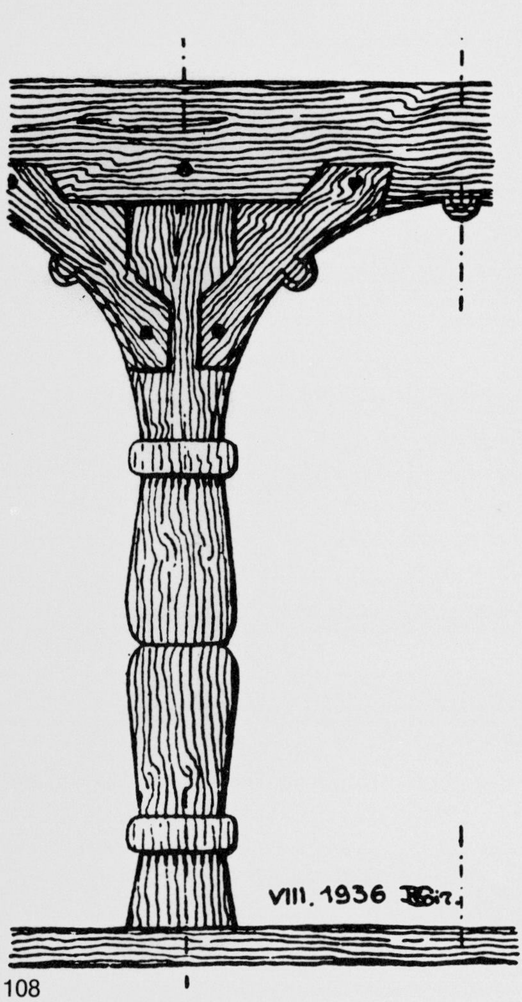

108 Pylypec'. Portalsäule, 1780.
Pylypec'. Porch column, 1780.

107

109

110

109 Izky. Kirche des Hl. Nikolaus, 1798 (1925).
Izky. Church of St. Nicholas, 1798 (1925).

111

111 Izky. Eingangsportal mit Ikonen, Kirche des Hl. Nikolaus, 1798 (1925).
Izky. Entry porch with icons, Church of St. Nicholas, 1798 (1925).

110 Izky. Glockenturm für die Kirche des Hl. Nikolaus, 1798 (1925).
Izky. Bell tower for the Church of St. Nicholas, 1798 (1925).

112

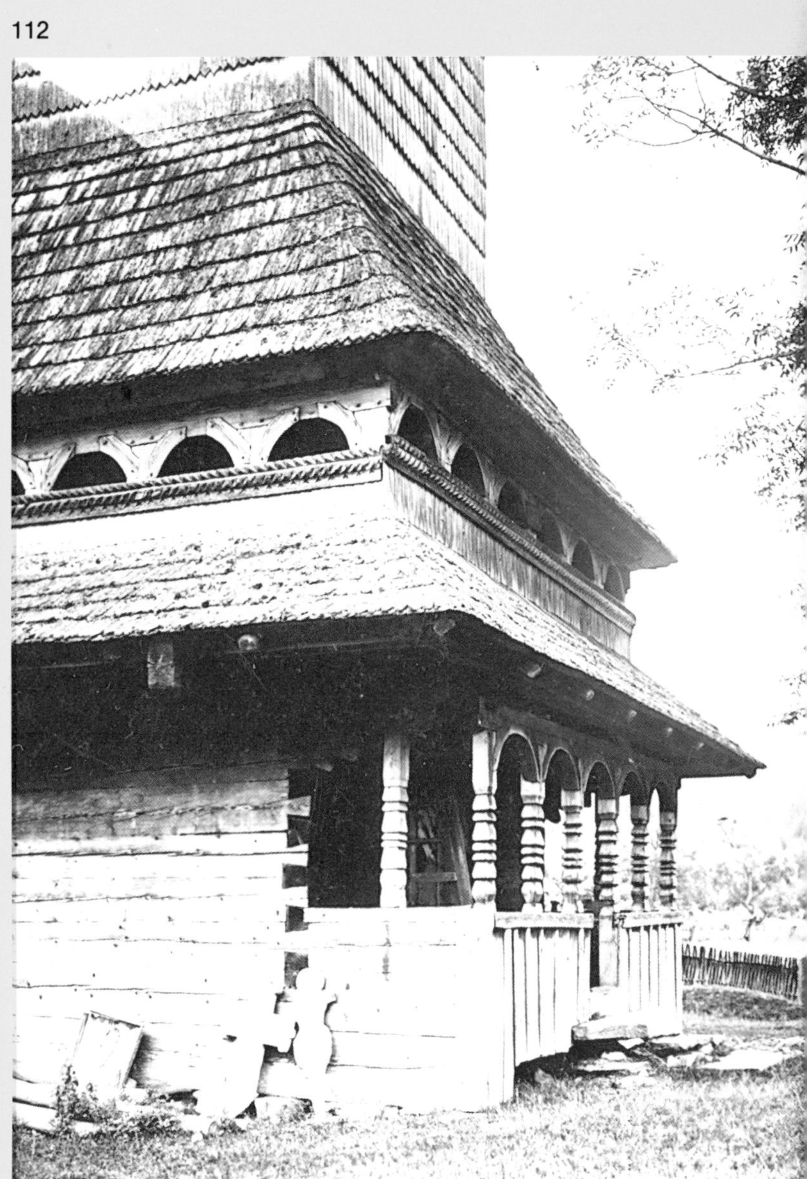

112 Verchnij Bystryj. Fassade, Kirche (1925).
Verchnij Bystryj. Façade, Church (1925).

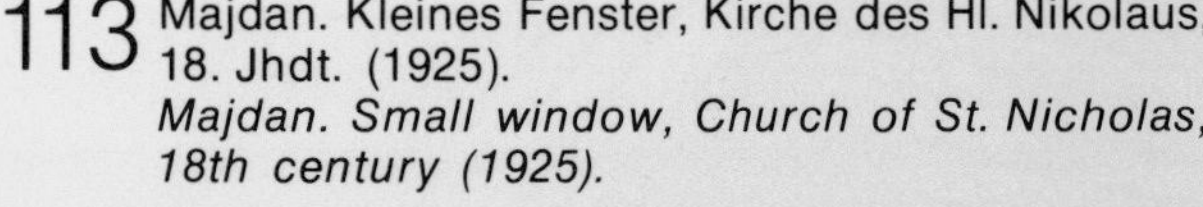

113 Majdan. Kleines Fenster, Kirche des Hl. Nikolaus, 18. Jhdt. (1925).
Majdan. Small window, Church of St. Nicholas, 18th century (1925).

114 Majdan. Eingang und Säulen, Kirche des Hl. Nikolaus, 18. Jhdt. (1925).
Majdan. Entrance and columns, Church of St. Nicholas, 18th century (1925).

113

114

115 Majdan. Portal (piddašok), Kirche des Hl. Nikolaus, 18. Jhdt. (1925).
Majdan. Porch (piddašok), Church of St. Nicholas, 18th century (1925).

116 Majdan. Tür, Kirche des Hl. Nikolaus, 18. Jhdt. (1925).
Majdan. Door, Church of St. Nicholas, 18th century (1925).

117 Majdan. Kirche des Hl. Nikolaus, 18. Jhdt. (1925).
Majdan. Church of St. Nicholas, 18th century (1925).

116

117

118

118 Ripynne. Haus (1925).
Ripynne. House (1925).

119 Ripynne. Holzbrücke (1925).
Ripynne. Wooden bridge (1925).

119

120 Ripynne. Kirche des Hl. Demitrius, 18. Jhdt. (1925).
Ripynne. Church of St. Demetrius, 18th century (1925).

121 Ripynne. Kirche des Hl. Demitrius, 18. Jhdt. (1925).
Ripynne. Church of St. Demetrius, 18th century (1925).

120

121

122

122 Tjuška. Fassade mit Galerie, Kirche des Hl. Nikolaus (1925).
Tjuška. Façade with gallery, Church of St. Nicholas (1925).

123 Prochudnyj. Eckbalken einer Scheune (1925).
Prochudnyj. Corner joints on a barn (1925).

124 Prochudnyj. Mineralbrunnen (1925).
Prochudnyj. Well for mineral water (1925).

123

124

125 Mižhirja (vormals Volove). Neuorthodoxe Kirche, 20. Jhdt. (1925).
Mižhirja (formerly Volove). New Orthodox Church, 20th century (1925).

125

126 Mižhirja (vormals Volove). Drei Generationen (1925).
Mižhirja (formerly Volovė). Three generations (1925).

127 Mižhirja (vormals Volove). Frau in Volkstracht (1925).
Mižhirja (formerly Volove). Woman in traditional dress (1925).

126

127

129 Mižhirja (vormals Volove), Großvater (1925).
Mižhirja (formerly Volove). Grandfather (1925).

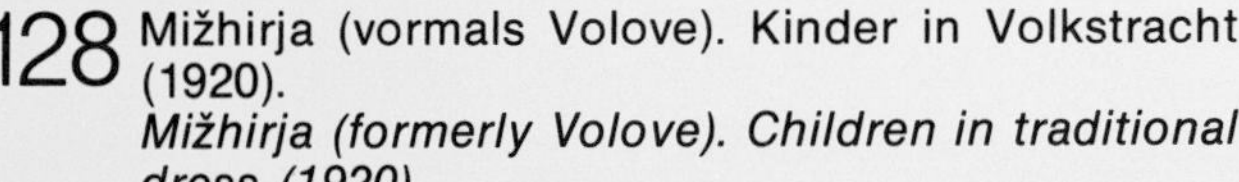

128 Mižhirja (vormals Volove). Kinder in Volkstracht (1920).
Mižhirja (formerly Volove). Children in traditional dress (1920).

129

128

130 Huklyvyj. Glockenturm für die Heilig-Geist-Kirche, 18. Jhdt. (1921).
Huklyvyj. Bell tower for the Church of the Holy Ghost, 18th century (1921).

131

131 Veretečiv. Glockenturm (1921).
Veretečiv. Bell tower (1921).

130

134 Huklyvyj. Eingangsportal, Heilig-Geist-Kirche, 18. Jhdt. (1921).
Huklyvyj. Entry porch, Church of the Holy Ghost, 18th century (1921).

132 Huklyvyj. Doppeltes Seitenfenster der Heilig-Geist-Kirche (1921).
Huklyvyj. Double window on side of Church of the Holy Ghost (1921).

133 Huklyvyj. Eckbalken, Heilig-Geist-Kirche, 18. Jhdt. (1921).
Huklyvyj. Corner joints, Church of the Holy Ghost, 18th century (1921).

132

133

134

135

135 Huklyvyj. Heilig-Geist-Kirche und Glockenturm, 18. Jhdt. (1921).
Huklyvyj. Church of the Holy Ghost and bell tower, 18th century (1921).

136 Huklyvyj. Heilig-Geist-Kirche, 18. Jhdt. (1921).
Huklyvyj. Church of the Holy Ghost, 18th century (1921).

137

138

137 Talamoš. ,,Kaiserliche Pforten" der früheren Kirche (1921).
Talamoš. "Royal Gates" from the former church (1921).

138 Talamoš. ,,Kaiserliche Pforten" der früheren Kirche (1921).
Talamoš. "Royal Gates" from the former church (1921).

139 Talamoš. Ikonenfragment der früheren Kirche (1921).
Talamoš. Fragment of icons from the former church (1921).

139

140 Talamoš. Ikone des Erzengels Gabriel der früheren Kirche (1921).
Talamoš. Icon of the Archangel Gabriel from the former church (1921).

141

141 Talamoš. Lesepulte der früheren Kirche (1921).
Talamoš. Book stands from the former church (1921).

140

142

142 Zadil's'kyj. Kirche des Hl. Nikolaus (1921).
Zadil's'kyj. Church of St. Nicholas (1921).

143 Tyšiv. Mariä Aufnahme in den Himmel, 1898 (1921).
Tyšiv. Church of the Assumption of the Blessed Virgin Mary, 1898 (1921).

143

144

144 Jalove. Kirche des Hl. Basilius und Glockenturm (1921).
Jalove. Church of St. Basil and bell tower (1921).

145 Jalove. Überdachte Veranda (piddašok) eines Hauses (1921).
Jalove. Covered porch (piddašok) of house (1921).

145

147 Ploske, Basengalerie um die Kirche Maria Fürsprecherin. In den 20er Jahren des 20. Jhdts. nach Kanora verlegt.
Ploske. Base gallery around Church of the Intercession of the Virgin, 1792 (1919). Transferred in the 1920's to Kanora.

146

14

146 Ploske. Kirche Maria Fürsprecherin, 1792 (1919). In den 20er Jahren des 20. Jhdts. nach Kanora verlegt.
Ploske. Church of the Intercession of the Virgin, 1792 (1919). Transferred in the 1920's to Kanora.

148 Ploske. Rückansicht, Kirche Maria Fürsprecherin, 1792 (1919). In den 20er Jahren des 20. Jhdts. nach Kanora verlegt.
Ploske. Rear view, Church of the Intercession of the Virgin, 1792 (1919). Transferred in the 1920's to Kanora.

149 Rozsoš (vormals Kopar). Fassade, Kirche des Erzengels Michael (1921).
Rozsoš (formerly Kopar) Façade, Church of St. Michael the Archangel (1921).

150 Rozsoš (vormals Kopar). Eingang, Kirche des Erzengels Michael (1921).
Rozsoš (formerly Kopar). Entrance, Church of the Archangel Michael (1921).

149

150

151

151 Rozsoš (vormals Kopar). Kirche des Erzengels Michael (1921).
Rozsoš (formerly Kopar). Church of the Archangel Michael (1921).

152

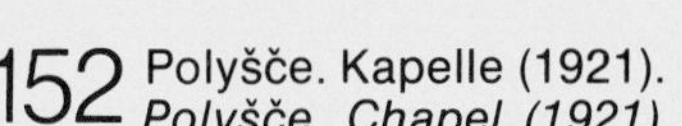

152 Polyšče. Kapelle (1921).
Polyšče. Chapel (1921).

154 Plavja. Kirche des Hl. Nikolaus (1921).
Plavja. Church of St. Nicholas (1921).

154

155 Plavja. Rückansicht, Kirche des Hl. Nikolaus (1921).
Plavja. Rear view, Church of St. Nicholas (1921).

153 Plavja. Eckbalken, Kirche des Hl. Nikolaus (1921).
Plavja. Corner joints, Church of St. Nicholas (1921).

153

156 Pasika. Haus (1920).
Pasika. House (1920).

156

157

157 Mukačevo. Haus (1919).
Mukačevo. House (1919).

158 Obava. Kirche Mariä Aufnahme in den Himmel, Anfang des 18. Jhdts. 1930 nach Nová Paka, Mähren, verlegt.
Obava. Church of the Assumption of the Blessed Virgin Mary, early 18th century. Transferred in 1930 to Nová Paka, Moravia.

158

159

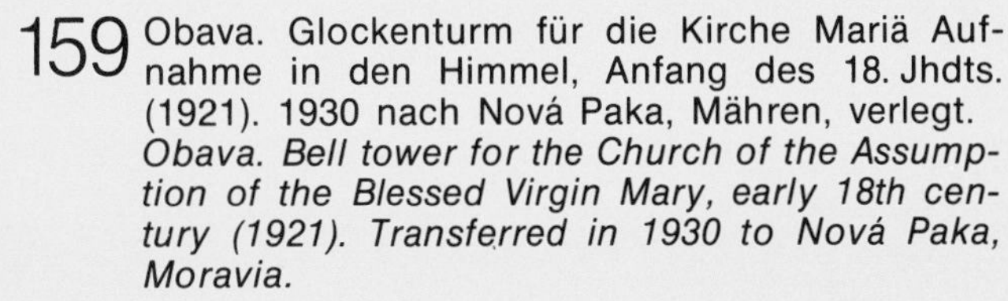

159 Obava. Glockenturm für die Kirche Mariä Aufnahme in den Himmel, Anfang des 18. Jhdts. (1921). 1930 nach Nová Paka, Mähren, verlegt.
Obava. Bell tower for the Church of the Assumption of the Blessed Virgin Mary, early 18th century (1921). Transferred in 1930 to Nová Paka, Moravia.

160 Kosyno. Ev. Kirche (1921).
Kosyno. Evangelical church (1921).

160

161

161 Kosyno. Friedhofskreuz (1921).
Kosyno. Cemetery cross (1921).

Hlynjanec'. Kirche des Erzengels Michael (1921). 1931 nach Kunčice in Mähren verlegt.
Hlynjanec'. Church of the Archangel Michael (1921). Transferred in 1931 to Kunčice in Moravia.

162

163

163 Hlynjanec'. Kirche des Erzengels Michael (1921). 1931 nach Kunčice in Mähren verlegt.
Hlynjanec'. Church of the Archangel Michael (1921). Transferred in 1931 to Kunčice in Moravia.

164

164 Nyžnja Vyžnycja. Kirche des Erzengels Michael (1921).
Nyžnja Vyžnycja. Church of the Archangel Michael (1921).

165 Nyžnja Vyžnycja. Rückansicht, Kirche des Erzengels Michael (1921).
Nyžnja Vyžnycja. Rear view, Church of the Archangel Michael (1921).

165

167 Šelestovo. Basengalerie um die Kirche des Erzengels Michael, 1777 (1921). 1927 nach Mukačevo verlegt.
Šelestovo. Base gallery around the Church of the Archangel Michael, 1777 (1921). Transferred to Mukačevo in 1927.

167

166 Hlynjanec'. Basengalerie um die Kirche des Erzengels Michael (1921). 1931 nach Kunčice in Mähren verlegt.
Hlynjanec'. Base gallery around the Church of the Archangel Michael (1921). Transferred in 1931 to Kunčice in Moravia.

166

168 Šelestovo. Kirche des Erzengels Michael, 1777 (1921). 1927 nach Mukačevo verlegt.
Šelestovo. Church of the Archangel Michael, 1777 (1921). Transferred to Mukačevo in 1927.

168

169 Užok. Kirche des Erzengels Michael, 1745 (1920).
Užok. Church of the Archangel Michael, 1745 (1920).

169

170

170 Užok. Überdachte Endbalken, Kirche des Erzengels Michael, 1745.
Užok. Covered end joints, Church of the Archangel Michael, 1745.

171

172

171 Husnyj. Männer in Volkstracht (1920).
Husnyj. Men in traditional dress (1920).

172 Husnyj. Der Dorfmüller (1920).
Husnyj. The village miller (1920).

173

173 Husnyj. Haus (1920).
Husnyj. House (1920).

174 Husnyj. Kirche des Hl. Nikolaus, 1759 (1920).
Husnyj. Church of St. Nicholas, 1759 (1920).

174

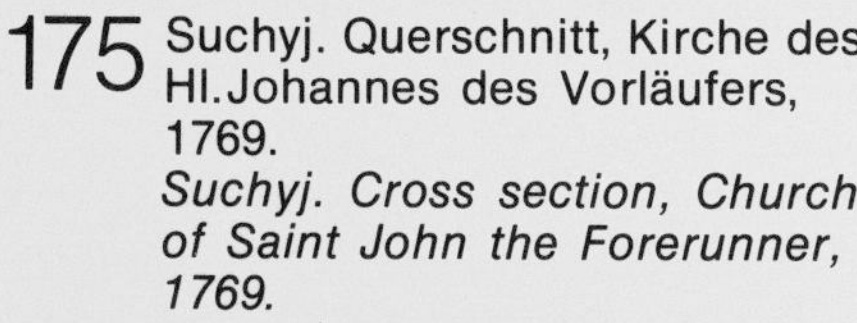

175 Suchyj. Querschnitt, Kirche des Hl.Johannes des Vorläufers, 1769.
Suchyj. Cross section, Church of Saint John the Forerunner, 1769.

175

176 Suchyj. Grundriß, Kirche des Hl. Johannes des Vorläufers, 1769.
Suchyj. Ground plan, Church of Saint John the Forerunner, 1769.

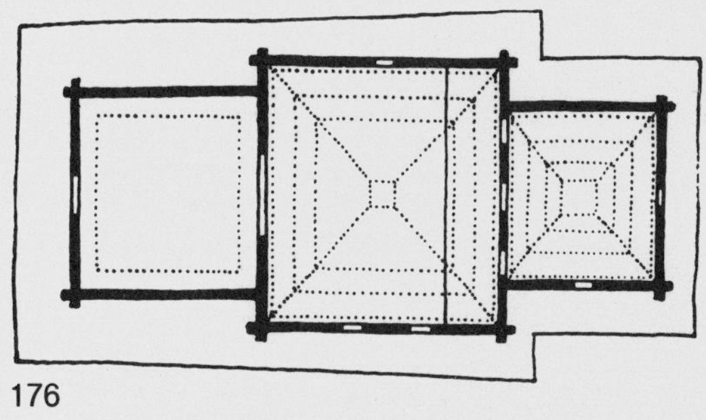

176

177 Suchyj. Kirche des Hl. Johannes des Vorläufers, 1769 (1925).
Suchyj. Church of St. John the Forerunner, 1769 (1925).

177

178

178 Suchyj. Glockenturm für die Kirche des Hl. Johannes des Vorläufers (1925).
Suchyj. Bell tower for the Church of St. John the Forerunner (1925).

179

180

179 Suchyj. Glockenturm und Kruzifix für die Kirche des Hl. Johannes des Vorläufers (1925).
Suchyj. Bell tower and crucifix for the Church of St. John the Forerunner (1925).

180 Suchyj. Kruzifix (1925).
Suchyj. Crucifix (1925).

181

182

181 Lubnja. „Kaiserliche Pforte“ (1921).
Lubnja. “Royal Gate” (1921).

182 Lubnja. Kirche (1921).
Lubnja. Church (1921).

183 Lubnja. Kirche (1921).
Lubnja. Church (1921).

183

184

184 Vyška. Fassade, Kirche des Erzengels Michael, 18. Jhdt. (1921).
Vyška. Façade, Church of the Archangel Michael, 18th century (1921).

185 Vyška. Rückansicht, Kirche des Erzengels Michael, 18. Jhdt. (1921).
Vyška. Rear view, Church of the Archangel Michael, 18th century (1921).

186 Vyška. Kirche des Erzengels Michael, 18. Jhdt. (1921).
Vyška. Church of the Archangel Michael, 18th century (1921).

185

186

187 Luh. Kruzifix (1921).
Luh. Crucifix (1921). 187

188 Kostryna. Hinterer Teil, Kirche Maria Fürsprecherin, 1761 (1920).
Kostryna. Rear portion, Church of the Intercession of the Virgin, 1761 (1920).

189 Nyžnja Roztoka. Stalltür (1925).
Nyžnja Roztoka. Stable door (1925).

188

189

190 Kostryna. Kirche Maria Fürsprecherin, 1761 (1920).
Kostryna. Church of the Intercession of the Virgin, 1761 (1920).

192

191 Sil'. Kirche des Hl. Basilius, 1777 (1921).
Sil'. Church of St. Basil, 1777 (1921).

192 Sil'. Eingang, Kirche des Hl. Basilius (1921).
Sil'. Entrance, Church of St. Basil (1921).

193 Sil'. Rückansicht, Kirche des Hl. Basilius, 1777 (1921).
Sil'. Rear view, Church of St. Basil, 1777 (1921).

191

193

194

194 Domašyn. Kirche des Erzengels Michael (1921).
Domašyn. Church of the Archangel Michael (1921).

196 Novoselycja/Nová Sedlica. Rückansicht, Kirche des Erzengels Michael, 1764 (1920).
Novoselycja/Nová Sedlica. Rear view, Church of the Archangel Michael, 1764 (1920).

195 Novoselycja/Nová Sedlica. Kirche des Erzengels Michael, 1764 (1920).
Novoselycja/Nová Sedlica. Church of the Archangel Michael, 1764 (1920).

195

197 Ulyč-Kryve/Uličské Krivé. Nordseite, Kirche des Erzengels Michael, 1. Hälfte des 18. Jhdts. (1925).
Ulyč-Kryve/Uličské Krivé. North side, Church of the Archangel Michael, first half of the 18th century (1925).

198 Ulyč-Kryve/Uličské Krivé. Kirche des Erzengels Michael, 1. Hälfte des 18. Jhdts. (1925).
Ulyč-Kryve/Uličské Krivé. Church of the Archangel Michael, first half of the 18th century (1925).

199 Zboj. Kirche des Hl. Nikolaus, 1766 (1921). 1967 nach Bardejovské Kúpele verlegt.
Zboj. Church of St. Nicholas, 1766 (1921). Transferred in 1967 to Bardejovské Kúpele.

200 Zboj. Rückansicht, Kirche des Hl. Nikolaus, 1766 (1921).
Zboj. Rear view, Church of St. Nicholas, 1766 (1921).

197

198

199

201

201 Čornoholova. Pforte, Kirche des Hl. Nikolaus (1921).
Čornoholova. Gate, Church of St. Nicholas (1921).

202 Kamjanycja. Mädchen in Volkstracht (1920).
Kamjanycja. Girl in traditional dress (1920).

203 Kamjanycja. Mann in Gebirgsmantel (1920).
Kamjanycja. Man in a mountaineer coat (1920).

204 Čornoholova. Rückansicht. Kirche des Hl. Nikolaus, 1794 (1921).
Čornoholova. Rear view, Church of St. Nicholas, 1794 (1921).

203

202

205 Horjany. Haus (1920).
Horjany. House (1920).

205

206

206 Horjany. Haus (1920).
Horjany. House (1920).

207

207 Horjany. Stall und Hühnerkäfig (1920).
Horjany. Stable and chicken coop (1920).

208

208 Horjany. Rundbau, 12. Jhdt. und Kirche, 14. Jhdt. (1921).
Horjany. Rotunda, 12th century, and church, 14th century (1921).

209

210

211

209 Ondavka. Marienkirche, 18. Jhdt. (1923). Zerstört.
Ondavka. Church of the Blessed Virgin Mary, 18th century (1923). Destroyed.

210 Ondavka. „Kaiserlicher Eingang", Marienkirche (1923). Zerstört.
Ondavka. "Royal entry", Church of the Blessed Virgin Mary (1923). Destroyed.

211 Ondavka. Fenster, Marienkirche, 18. Jhdt. (1923). Zerstört.
Ondavka. Window, Church of the Blessed Virgin Mary, 18th century (1923). Destroyed.

212 Ondavka. Pforte, Marienkirche, 18. Jhdt. (1923). Zerstört.
Ondavka. Gate, Church of the Blessed Virgin Mary, 18th century (1923). Destroyed.

212

213 Nyžnja Poljanka/Nižná Polianka. Kreuz der Kirche der Hl. Kuzma und Demjan (1923). Im 1. Weltkrieg zerstört.
Nyžnja Poljanka/Nižná Polianka. Cross from the Church of Sts. Kuzma and Demjan (1923). Destroyed during the First World War.

214 Jalynka/Jedlinka. Marienkirche, 1763 (1923).
Jalynka/Jedlinka. Church of the Blessed Virgin Mary, 1763 (1923).

213

214

216 Mikulašova / Mikulášova. Fassade, Marienkirche, Anfang des 18. Jhdts. (1923).
Mikulašova / Mikulášova. Façade, Church of the Blessed Virgin Mary, early 18th century (1923).

216

215 Mikulašova/Mikulášova (vormals Niklova). Marienkirche, Anfang des 18. Jhdts., 1837 vergrößert (1923). 1926 nach Bardejovské Kúpele verlegt.
Mikulašova/Mikulášova (formerly Niklova). Church of the Blessed Virgin Mary, early 18th century, enlarged 1837 (1923). Transferred in 1926 to Bardejovské Kúpele.

215

218 Nyžnij Myrošiv/Nižný Mirošov. Pforte, Kirche der Hl. Kuzma und Demjan (1923).
Nyžnij Myrošiv/Nižný Mirošov. Gate, Church of Sts. Kuzma and Demjan (1923).

218

217

217 Nyžnij Myrošiv/Nižný Mirošov. Hauptkuppel, Kirche de Hl. Kuzma und Demjan (1923). Im 1. Weltkrieg beschädig und später abgebaut.
Nyžnij Myrošiv/Nižný Mirošov. Central dome, Church c Sts. Kuzma and Demjan (1923). Damaged during First Worl War and later dismantled.

219 Nyžnij Orlyk/Nižný Orlik. Glockenturm der Kirche des Erzengels Michael, 18. Jhdt. (1923). Im 2. Weltkrieg zerstört. Modell rekonstruiert, im Museum zu Bardejovské Kúpele.
Nyžnij Orlyk/Nižný Orlik. Bell tower for the Church of the Archangel Michael, 18th century (1923). Destroyed during Second World War. Copy reconstructed in Museum at Bardejovské Kúpele.

219

220

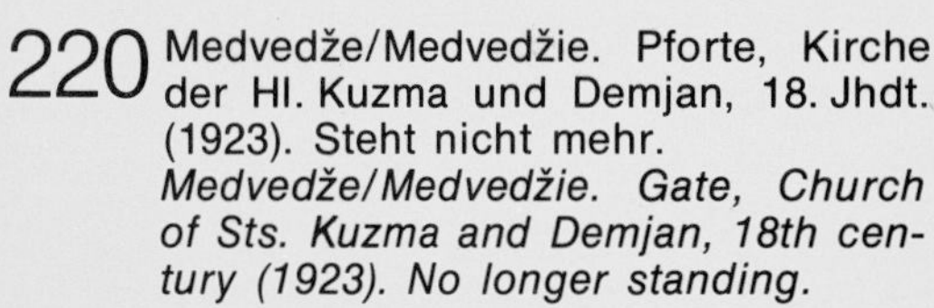

220 Medvedže/Medvedžie. Pforte, Kirche der Hl. Kuzma und Demjan, 18. Jhdt. (1923). Steht nicht mehr.
Medvedže/Medvedžie. Gate, Church of Sts. Kuzma and Demjan, 18th century (1923). No longer standing.

221

221 Nyžnij Orlyk/Nižný Orlik. Kuppeln, Kirche des Erzengels Michael, 18. Jhdt. (1923). Im 2. Weltkrieg zerstört.
Nyžnij Orlyk/Nižný Orlik. Domes, Church of the Archangel Michael, 18th century (1923). Destroyed during Second World War.

222

222 Nyžnij Orlyk/Nižný Orlik. Kirche des Erzengels Michael, 18. Jhdt. (1923). Im 2. Weltkrieg zerstört.
Nyžnij Orlyk/Nižný Orlik. Church of the Archangel Michael, 18th century (1923). Destroyed during Second World War.

223 Korejivci/Korejovce. Marienkirche, 1764 (1923).
Korejivci/Korejovce. Church of the Blessed Virgin Mary, 1764 (1923).

223

224 Korejivci/Korejovce. Marienkirche und Kruzifix, 1764 (1923).
Korejivci/Korejovce. Church of the Blessed Virgin Mary and crucifix, 1764 (1923).

224

225 Korejivci/Korejovce. Rückansicht, Marienkirche, 1764 (1923).
Korejivci/Korejovce. Rear view, Church of the Blessed Virgin Mary, 1764 (1923).

225

226

226 Kružlová. Fenster auf der Nordseite, Michaelskirche, Mitte des 17. Jhdts. (1923). Abgebaut während der 30er Jahre des 20. Jhdts.
Kružlová. Window on north side, Church of St. Michael, mid-17th century (1923). Dismantled during 1930's.

227 Kružlová. Michaelskirche, Mitte des 17. Jhdts. (1923). In den 30er Jahren des 20. Jhdts. abgebaut.
Kružlová. Church of St. Michael, mid-17th century (1923). Dismantled during 1930's.

227

228 Krajnje Čorne/Krajne Čierne. Pforte. Kirche des Hl. Basilius des Märtyrers, Mitte des 18. Jhdts. (1923).
Krajnje Čorne/Krajné Čierne. Gate. Church of St. Basil the Martyr, mid-18th century (1923).

228

229

229 Krajnje Čorne/Krajne Čierne. Rückansicht, Kirche des Hl. Basilius des Märtyrers, Mitte des 18. Jhdts. (1923).
Krajnje Čorne/Krajné Čierne. Rear view, Church of St. Basil the Martyr, mid-18th century (1923).

230

230 Ladomyrova/Ladomirová. Hintere Kuppel. Kirche des Erzengels Michael, 1742 (1923).
Ladomyrova/Ladomirová. Rear dome, Church of the Archangel Michael, 1742 (1923).

231 Ladomyrova/Ladomirová. Kuppeln, Kirche des Erzengels Michael, 1742 (1923).
Ladomyrova/Ladomirová. Domes, Church of the Archangel Michael, 1742 (1923).

231

232

232 Bogljarka. Kapelle (1923).
Bogljarka. Chapel (1923).

233

233 Kryve/Krivé. Kirche des Hl. Lukas, 1826 (1923).
Kryve/Krivé. Church of St. Luke, 1826 (1923).

234 Andrijova/Andrejová. Teil alter Kirche, 1882 abgebrannt (1923). Steht nicht mehr.
Andrijova/Andrejova. Part of old church, burned in 1882 (1923). No longer standing.

235 Biloveža/Beloveža. Michaelskirche, 1778, 1898 wieder aufgebaut (1923).
Biloveža/Beloveža. Church of St. Michael, 1778, rebuilt 1898 (1923).

234

235

236

236 Biloveža/Beloveža. Kuppeln, Michaelskirche, 1778, 1898 wieder aufgebaut (1923).
Biloveža/Beloveža. Domes, Church of St. Michael, 1778, rebuilt 1898 (1923).

237 Biloveža/Beloveža. Kuppeln, Michaelskirche, 1778, 1898 wieder aufgebaut (1923).
Biloveža/Beloveža. Domes, Church of St. Michael, 1778, rebuilt 1898 (1923).

237

238 Kožany. Marienkirche, 2. Hälfte des 18. Jhdts. (1923).
Kožany. Church of the Blessed Virgin Mary, second half 18th century (1923).

239 Kožany. Nordseite, Marienkirche, 2. Hälfte des 18. Jhdts. (1923).
Kožany. North side, Church of the Blessed Virgin Mary, second half 18th century (1923).

238

239

240 Kožany. Marienkirche, 2. Hälfte des 18. Jhdts. (1923).
Kožany. Church of the Blessed Virgin Mary, second half 18th century (1923).

241 Šarys'kyj Ščavnyk/Šarišský Štiavnik. Kirche, 1773 (1923). 1928 abgebaut.
Šarys'kyj Ščavnyk/Šarišský Štiavnik. Church, 1773 (1923). Dismantled 1928.

242

242 Šapynec'/Šapinec. Brunnen (1923).
Šapynec'/Šapinec. Well (1923).

243 Šarys'kyj Ščavnyk/Šarišský Štiavnik, Kirche, 1773 (1923). 1928 abgebaut.
Šarys'kyj Ščavnyk/Šarišský Štiavnik, Church, 1773 (1923). Dismantled 1928.

241

243

245 Točany. Querschnitt, Kirche des Hl. Lukas, 1739.
Trocany. Cross section, Church of St. Luke, 1739.

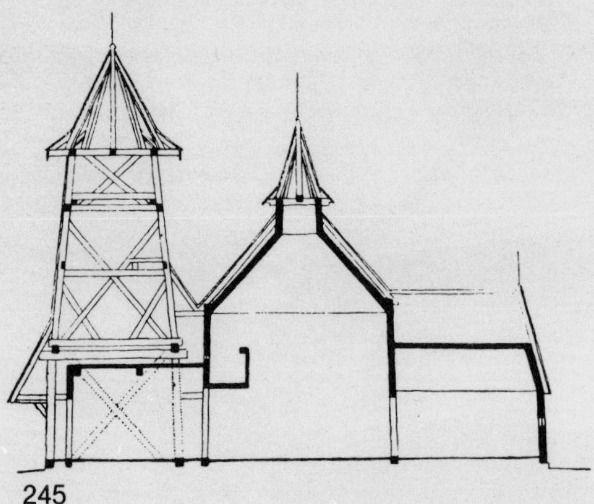

245

246 Trocany. Grundriß, Kirche des Hl. Lukas, 1739.
Trocany. Ground plan, Church of St. Luke, 1739.

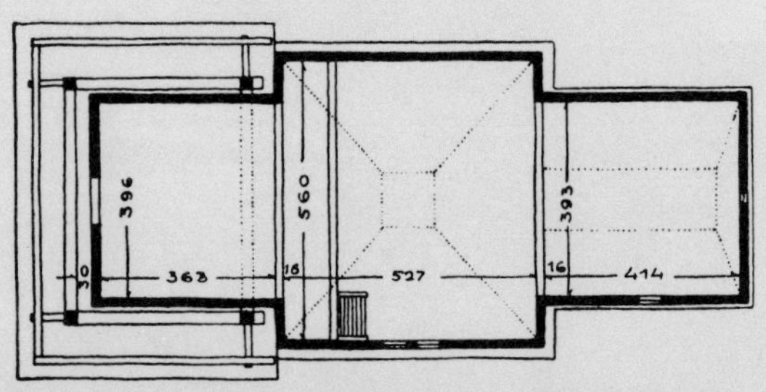

246

244

248

247

248 Tročany. Tür, Kirche des Hl. Lukas, 1739 (1923).
Tročany. Door, Church of St. Luke, 1739 (1923).

247 Tročany. Rückensicht, Kirche des Hl. Lukas, 1739 (1923).
Tročany. Rear section, Church of St. Luke, 1739 (1923).

244 Tročany. Kirche des Hl. Lukas, 1739 (1923).
Tročany. Church of St. Luke, 1739 (1923).

ORTSREGISTER

(Namen in Klammern bezeichnen Flußtäler; Namen nach Querstrichen sind die slowakische Form für Dörfer, die im Nordosten Slowakiens liegen; Zahlen beziehen sich auf Abbildungen.)

INDEX

(Names in parentheses indicate river valleys; names after slashes are the Slovak form for villages located in northeastern Slovakia; numbers refer to illustrations.)

POLAND
CZECHOSLOVAKIA
HUNGARY
U. S. S.
0 5 10 15
0 20 km.
Ondavka
Jedlinka
Nyžnja Poljanka
Nižný Mirošov
Medvedzie
Korejovce
Mikulášová
Kružlová
Krajné Čierne
Bardejovské Kupelé
Andrejová
Nižný Orlík
Ladomirová
Svidník
Medzilaborce
Krivé
Bogljarka
Bardejov
Beloveža
Kožany
Stropkov
Šarišský Štiavnik
Šapinec
Tročany
Giraltovce
Sekčov
Prešov
Torysa
Košice
Hornad
Abauj-Torna
Zemplin
Šariš
Ondava
Toplja
Laborec
Humenné
Michalovce
Snina
Bodrog
Tysa
San
Nová Sedlica
Zboj
Lubnja
Užok
Ulićské Krivé
Domašyn
Luh
Vyška
Husnyj
Sil'
Kostryna
Nyžnja Roztoka
Suchyj
Velykyj Bereznyj
Čornoholova
Ljuta
Už
Perečyn
Kamjanycja
Horjany
Užhorod
Čop
Stryj
Tyšiv
Zadil's'kyj
Jalove
Polyšče
Talamoš
Kanora
Huklyvyj
Podobo
Ploske
Veča
Svaljava
Nyžnja Vyžnycja
Obava
Kosyno
Pasika
Hlynjanec'
Plavja
Rozsoš
Šelestovo
Latorycja
Mukačevo
Bereg
Kid'ovš
Boržava
Ugoča
Berehovo
Mužijevo
Vynohradiv (Sevljuš)
Olešnyk
Nove Selo
Pidvynohradiv
Verja
Četovo
Batar
Cholmec
Julivci
Szatmár
International boundaries
Historic county (župa) boundaries
Northeastern boundary of Czechoslovakia (1919-1939) and present-day boundary of Transcarpathian Oblast of the Ukrainian S.S.R.
Location of photographs in album
Other towns or cities